C000234171

CONTEN

REFERENCE

Motorway	M69	Cycleway (Selected)	🚲
		Church or Chapel	†
A Road	A5	Fire Station	■
B Road	B4114	Hospital	Ⓗ
Dual Carriageway		House Numbers A & B Roads only	22 48
One Way Street Traffic flow on A roads is also indicated by a heavy line on the driver's left.	→ →	Information Centre	ℹ
		National Grid Reference	^{4}00
Restricted Access		Police Station	▲
Pedestrianized Road		Post Office	★
Track & Footpath		Viewpoint	✳
Railway	Level Crossing / Station / Tunnel / Heritage Station	Toilet: without facilities for the Disabled with facilities for the Disabled	▽ ▽
Built Up Area	FARM / CL	Educational Establishment	⬛
Local Authority Boundary		Hospital or Hospice	⬛
Posttown Boundary		Industrial Building	⬜
Postcode Boundary within Posttowns		Leisure or Recreational Facility	⬛
		Place of Interest	⬛
Map Continuation	4	Public Building	⬛
		Shopping Centre or Market	⬛
Car Park (Selected)	P	Other Selected Buildings	⬜

SCALE

1:15,840   4 inches (10.16 cm) to 1 mile   6.31 cm to 1 km

0	¼	½	¾	1 Mile

0	250	500	750 Metres	1 Kilometre

Copyright of Geographers' A-Z Map Company Limited

Head Office :
Fairfield Road, Borough Green, Sevenoaks, Kent TN15 8PP
Tel: 01732 781000 (Enquiries & Trade Sales)
 01732 783422 (Retail Sales)
www.a-zmaps.co.uk

Ordnance Survey® This product includes mapping data licensed from Ordnance Survey®
with the permission of The Controller of Her Majesty's Stationery Office.

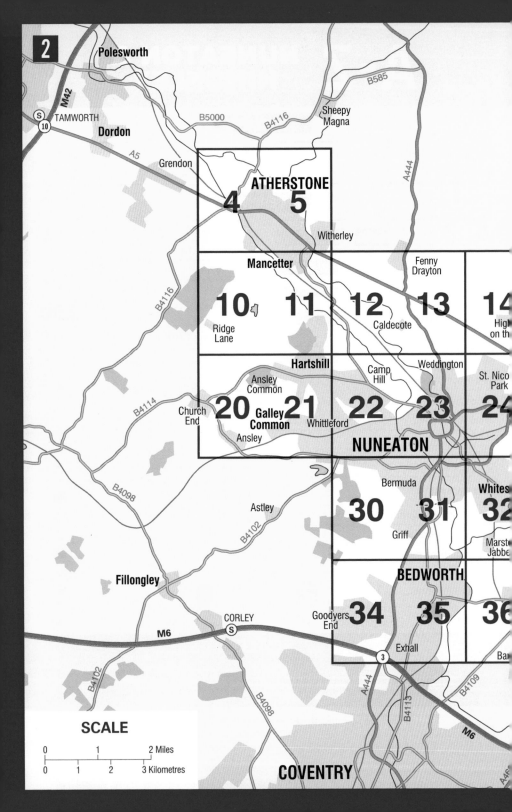

2

Polesworth

TAMWORTH

Dordon

Grendon

ATHERSTONE

4 **5**

Sheepy
Magna

Witherley

Mancetter

Fenny
Drayton

10 **11** **12** **13** **14**

Ridge
Lane

Caldecote

High
on th

Hartshill

Camp
Hill

Weddington

St. Nico
Park

Ansley
Common

Church
End

20 Galley **21** **22** **23** **24**
Common Whittleford

Ansley

NUNEATON

Bermuda

Whites

Astley

30 **31** **32**

Griff

Marst
Jabbe

Fillongley

BEDWORTH

CORLEY

Goodyers
End

34 **35** **36**

M6

Exhall

Ba

SCALE

0   1   2 Miles

0   1   2   3 Kilometres

COVENTRY

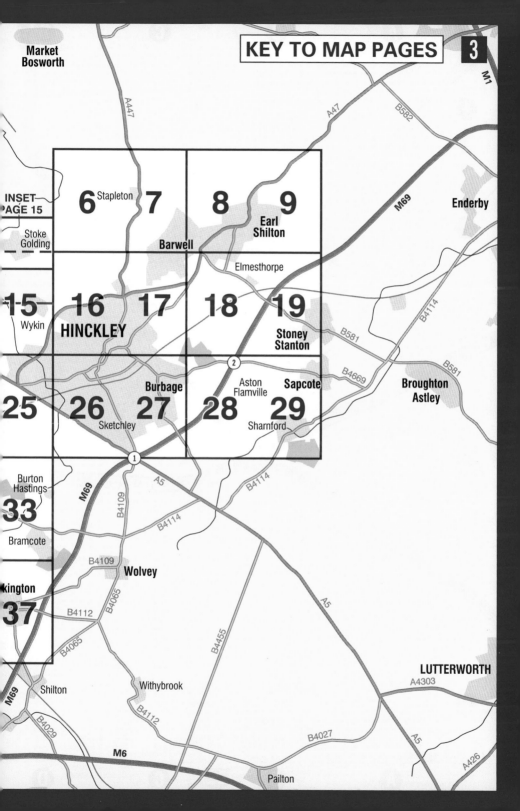

Market Bosworth

M1

A447

A47

B582

M69

Enderby

INSET PAGE 15

Stoke Golding

6 Stapleton   **7**

8   **9** Earl Shilton

Barwell

Elmesthorpe

B4114

15

Wykin

16 HINCKLEY   **17**

18   **19**

Stoney Stanton

B581

B4114

B4669

B581

Broughton Astley

25

26 Sketchley   **27** Burbage

28 Aston Flamville   **29** Sapcote

Sharnford

2

1

Burton Hastings

33

Bramcote

M69

B4109

A5

B4114

B4109

...kington

37

B4112

B4065

B4065

B4112

Wolvey

B4455

A5

LUTTERWORTH

A4303

M69

B4029

Shilton

Withybrook

B4027

A5

A426

M6

Pailton

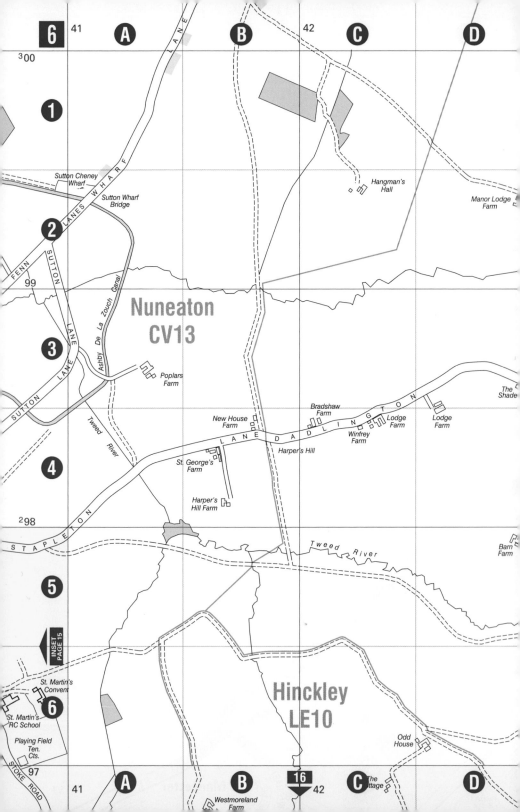

1

Sutton Cheney
Wharf

LANES WHARF

Sutton Wharf
Bridge

Hangman's
Hall

Manor Lodge
Farm

2

FENN

SUTTON LANE

ASHBY DE LA ZOUCH CANAL

99

**Nuneaton
CV13**

3

SUTTON LANE

Poplars
Farm

Bradshaw
Farm

The
Shade

New House
Farm

Lodge
Farm

Lodge
Farm

Winfrey
Farm

DADLINGTON LANE

Tweed River

Harper's Hill

4

St. George's
Farm

Harper's
Hill Farm

²98

STAPLETON

Tweed River

Barn
Farm

5

INSET
PAGE 15

St. Martin's
Convent

**Hinckley
LE10**

6

St. Martin's
RC School

Odd
House

Playing Field
Ten.
Cts.

STOKE ROAD

97

The
Cottage

Westmoreland
Farm

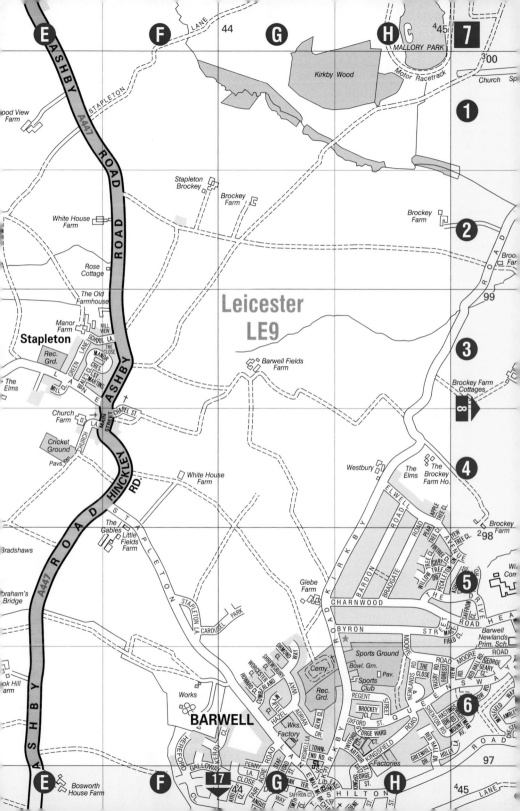

E Tooley Spinneys
F Tooley Park Cottages 48
G Works
H 49 **9**

3 00

Knoll Spinney

1

A47 ROAD

North Lodge

Bassett Farm

2

Long Spinneys

Tooley Farm

The Spinneys

99

Ash Spinney

Riverside Cottages

3 Normanton Turville

Upper Pool

Bracknell Farm

HINCKLEY & BOSWORTH HILL BLABY

Works

Nock Verges

Church Fm.

STREET THURLASTON

SHILTON

EARL

Normanton House Farm

Little Spinney

Normanton Hall

4

Normanton Park

298

ROAD

CHAPEL LANE

POPLARS

St. Peter's RC Prim. Sch.

BOSWORTH LINK

KING RICHARD'S HILL

ROMAN STREET

AVENUE

MONTGOMERY RD.

Cemy.

The Elms

WOLF WRIGHT CT. BOLTON CL. FRANK

GRN

Oakfield

LANE

Lower Pool

EARL AVENUE

TOM EATOUGH CT.

RONALD TOM RD.

MONTGOMERY RD.

RD. SOUTH

laying Field

LANE MILL

BullPit Farm

5

NARBOROUGH LA.

POTLERS LA.

Sewage Works

Mirfield Farm

Hillview

6

Yennards Lodge

The Yennards

97

E LANE
F Huit Farm
19 48
G
H 49

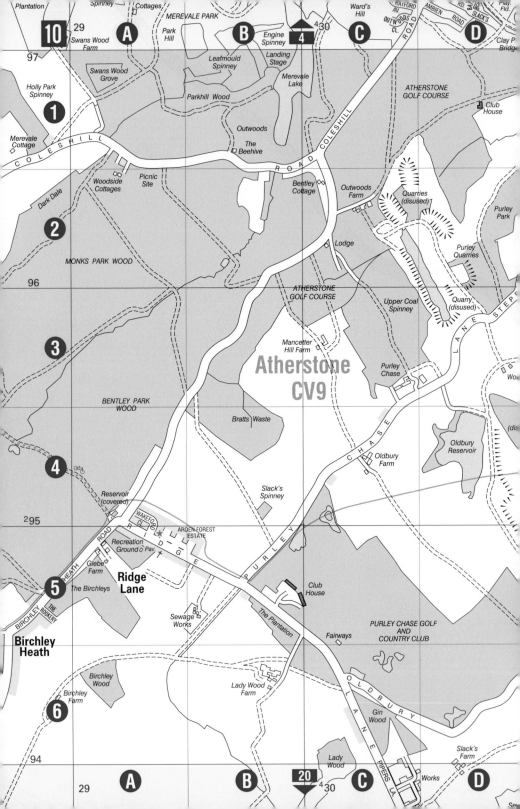

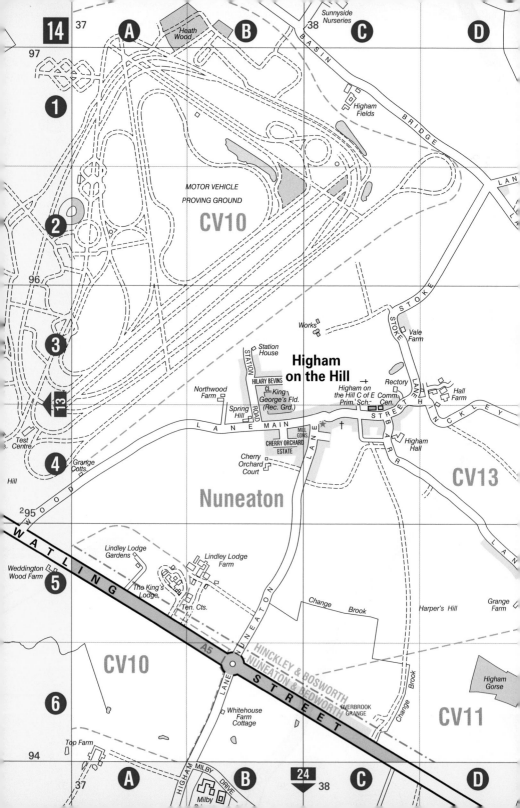

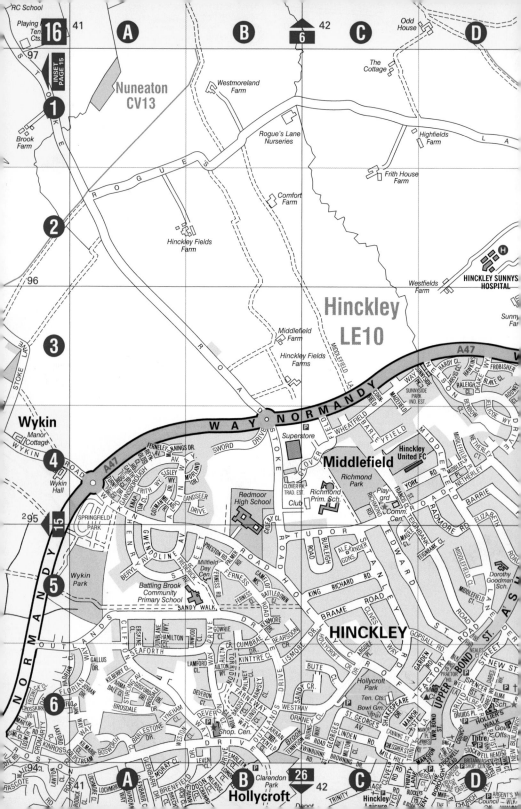

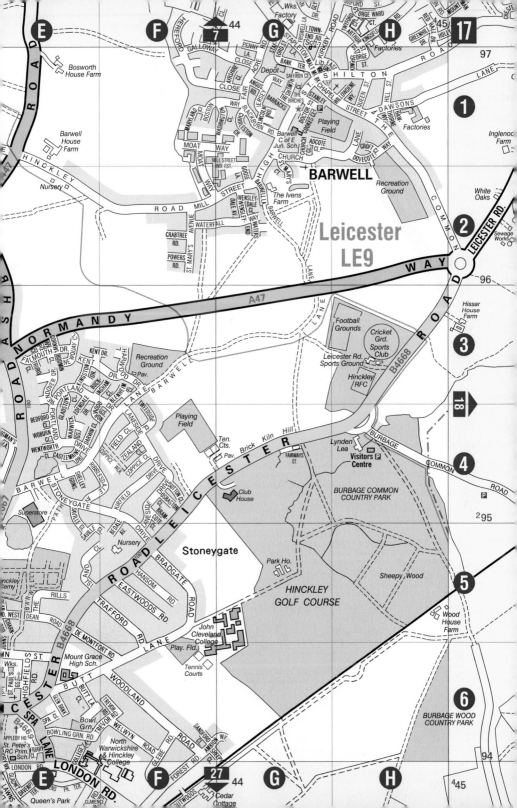

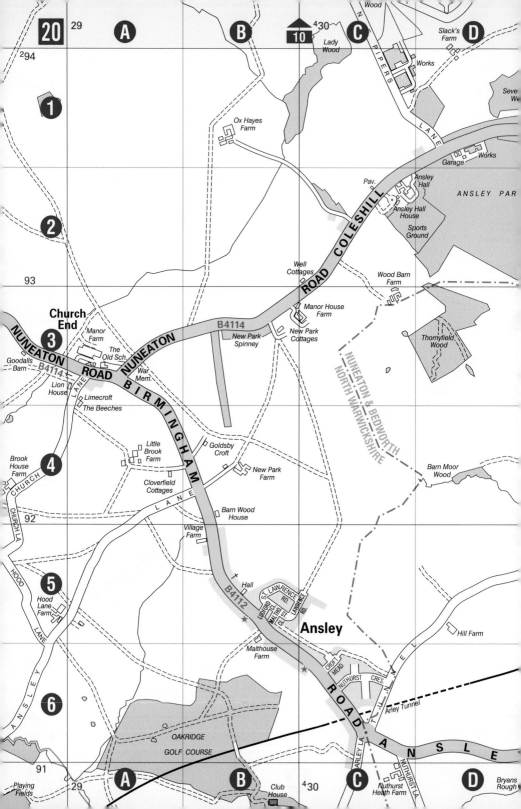

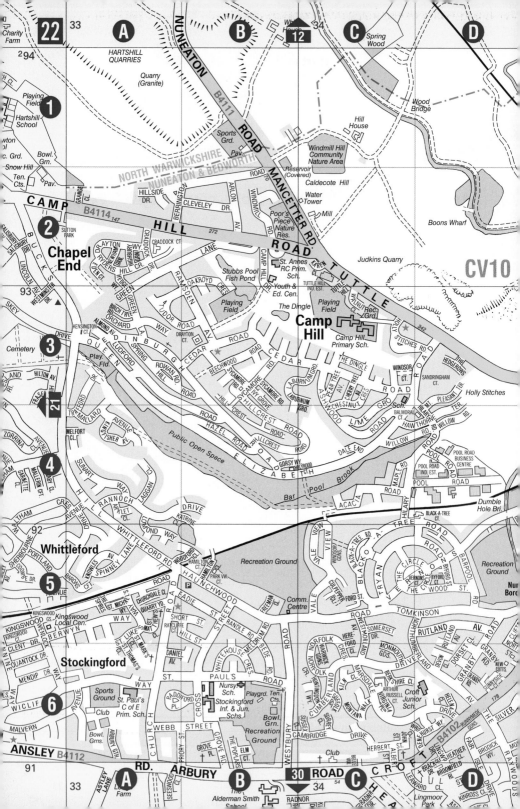

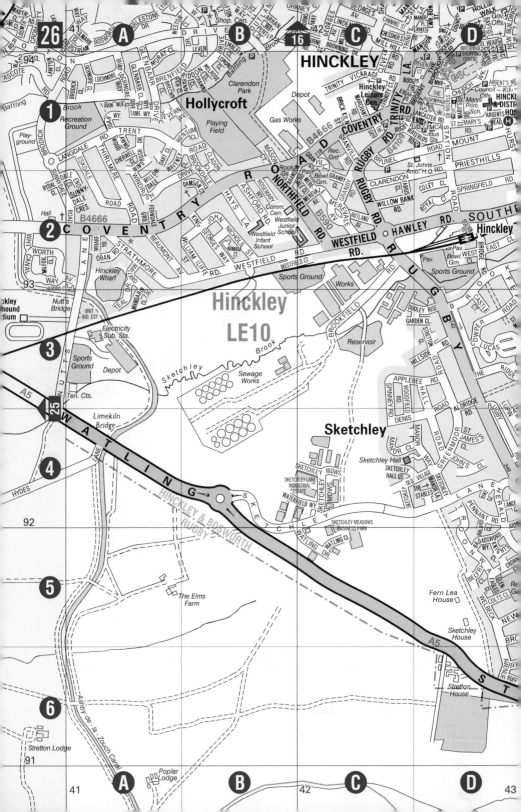

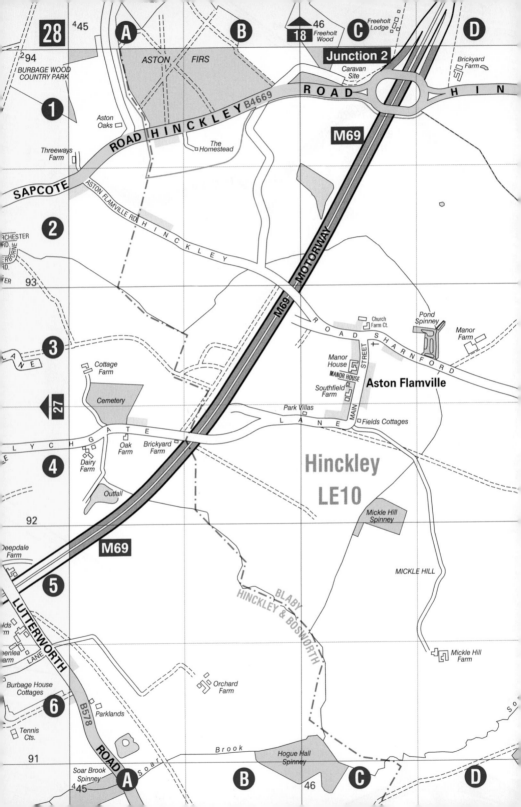

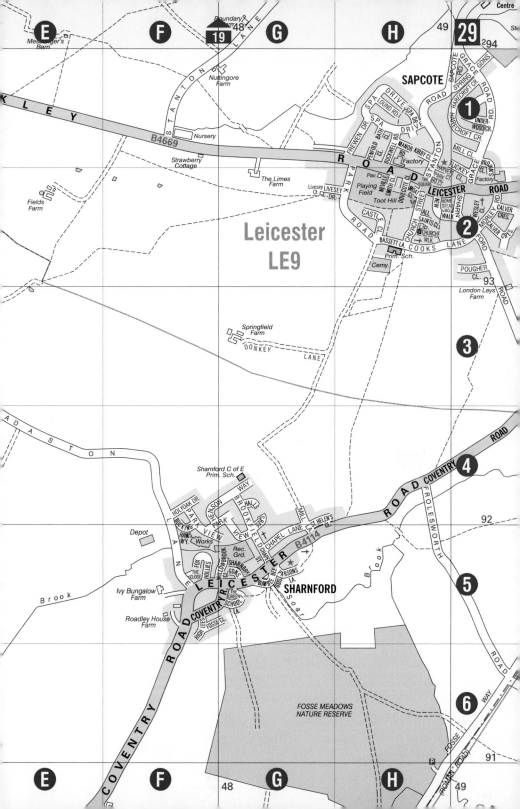

E   F   G   H   49   294   Centre

19   48   Boundary Farm

SAPCOTE

1

Messenger's Barn

Nuttingore Farm

GRACE GDNS.
SPRING RD.
GRACE ROAD
SAPCOTE ROAD
HARECROFT DR.
UNDER-WOOD CR.
HARECROFT CR.

FREWEN DR.
SPA DRIVE
LOUND RD.
SPA DRIVE
PENFOLD CL.
BATH
BUCKWELL
SMITH CL.
MANOR RD.
KIRBY CL.
Factory
MILL CL.
BROWN CL.

Nursery

B4669

STANTON LANE

Strawberry Cottage

The Limes Farm

ROAD

Livesey LIVESEY Ct. DR.

Pav. Field
Playing Field
Toot Hill

NEWBLE
NEWBLE CL.
DOVECOTE CL.
WM.
CHURCH STREET
ALL SAINTS CL.
CH. CHURCH
WLK.
SHAN
WALK
HOME STEAD
FORD
WESLEY CL.
MORLEY RD.
CALVER CRES.
CALVER CRES.

HARVEST
PARK CT.
THE SQUARE

LEICESTER **ROAD**

2

PARK ROAD

CASTLE CT.
BASSETT LA.
COOKS LANE
SHAN LANE

Prim. Sch.
Cemy.

POUGHER CL.
93
London Leys Farm

Leicester LE9

Fields Farm

Springfield Farm

DONKEY LANE

3

ADASTON LANE

ROAD
COVENTRY
FROLESWORTH ROAD

4
92

Sharnford C of E Prim. Sch.

HOLYOAK DR.
PARK VIEW
STEVENSON WAY
HALS
BROOKFIELD
MILL LANE
CHAPEL LANE
St. HELEN'S CL.

BUCKINGHAMS WY.
FOX LA.
WILLOWBROOK
THE HOLLIES
THE CLOSE
Works
Rec. Grd.
SHARNFORD ST.
GDNS.
BUMBLE BEE LA.
PARSONS
B4114
Brook

Depot

SHARNFORD

5

Ivy Bungalow Farm

Roadley House Farm

ROAD COVENTRY
LEICESTER
HIGH LEYS
FOSSE CL.
THE GREEN
SCHOOL LA.

Soar

FOSSE ROAD
PRIMARY ROAD

6
91

FOSSE MEADOWS NATURE RESERVE

P

E   F   48   G   H   49

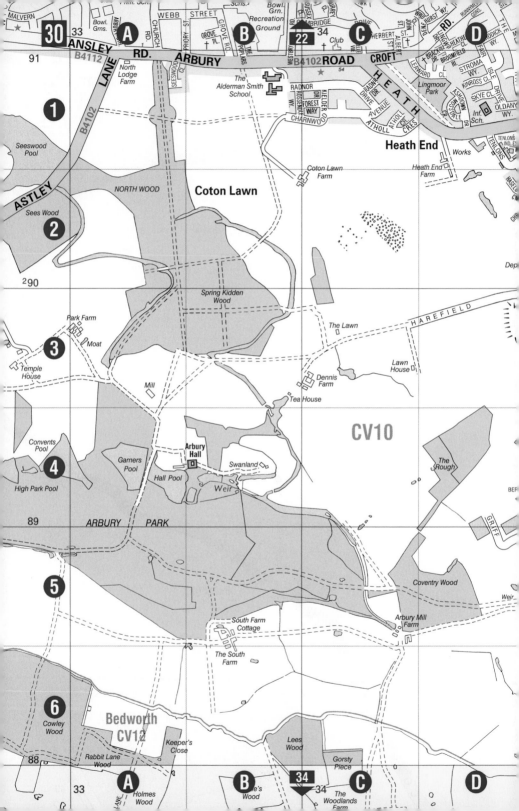

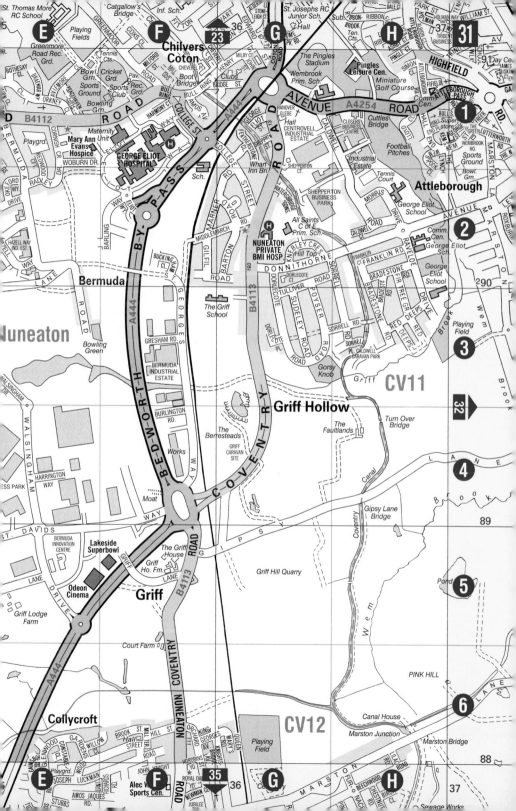

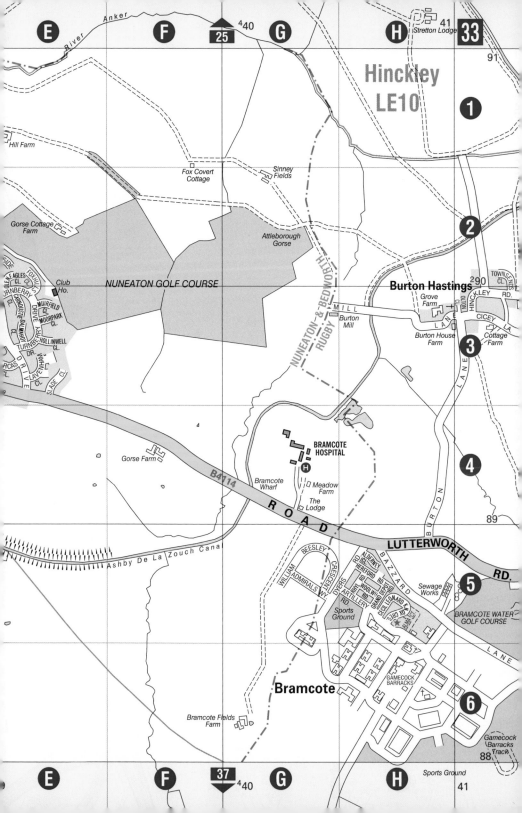

Hinckley LE10

1

Hill Farm

Fox Covert Cottage

Sinney Fields

2

Gorse Cottage Farm

Attleborough Gorse

EAGLES CL.
FOXHILL
SLADE
CL.
URNBERRY
CL.
CARNOUSTIE
DALMAHOY
Club Ho.
MUIRFIELD CL.
MOORPARK CL.
DRIVE
CL.
HOLLINWELL CL.
TURNBERRY
DR.
RCAS
WHARF
DRIVE
LAVENHAM
CL.
SLADE CL.

NUNEATON GOLF COURSE

NUNEATON & BEDWORTH
RUGBY

MILL
LANE
Burton Mill

Burton Hastings

Grove Farm

290
TOWNSEND
CL.
HINCKLEY RD.
CICEY
CICEY LA.

Burton House Farm

3

Cottage Farm

4

BRAMCOTE HOSPITAL

Bramcote Wharf

B4114

Gorse Farm

Meadow Farm

The Lodge

89

ROAD

BURTON
LANE

LUTTERWORTH
RD.

Ashby De La Zouch Canal

BEESLEY
WILLIAM
ADMIRALS
CRESCENT
DYERS
ALDERNEY RD.
HEREFORD
RD.
WOOLWICH RD.
BAZARD
ARTILLERY RD.
GRAND DEPOT
CECIL LEONARD RD.
CHICHESTER

Sports Ground

Sewage Works

5

BRAMCOTE WATER
GOLF COURSE

LANE

GAMECOCK
BARRACKS

Bramcote

6

Bramcote Fields Farm

Gamecock Barracks Track

88

Sports Ground

This is a map of Bedworth.

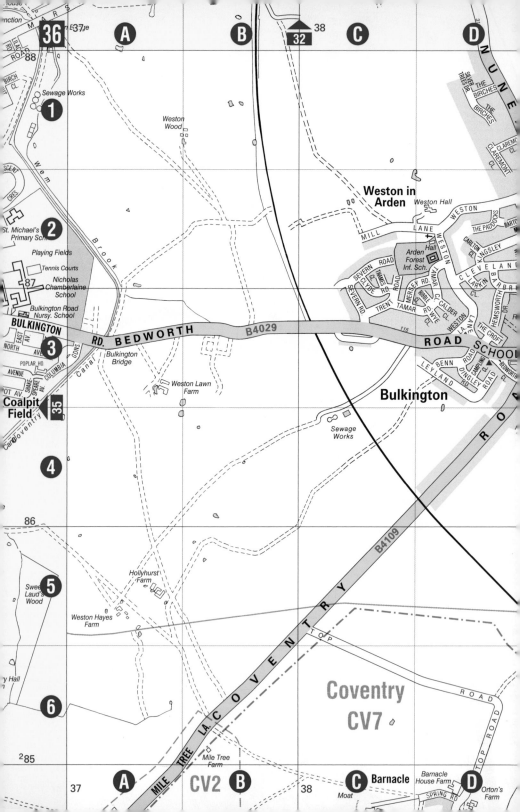

E   F   33 ⁴40   G   H   41   37   Gamecock Barracks Track
                                                          88
GAMECOCK
BARRACKS

Bramcote Fields
Farm

**Nuneaton
CV11**   1

**Bedworth
CV12**

M69   2

**Bramcote
Mains**   ROAD
                                                          87

Ryton

Hall Grounds
Farm

B4109   3

Ryton Farm
Bungalow

The Elms

B4112   ROAD

Arbury Bungalow
Farm

Arbury
House Farm   4

Well Green
Farm

Arbury
Cottage

Galley Hill
Fields

Arbury
House Farm   86

Bulkington
Fields Farm

Brook

Wern   5

Wolvey
Gorse

The Furlongs
Farm

SHILTON LA.
IND. EST.

M69   ROAD

B4065   6   Shilton Fields
                                                                        Farm
Lovitts
Farm   Shilton Fields

E   F   ⁴40   G   H   41   ²85

INDEX

Including Streets, Places & Areas, Hospitals & Hospices, Industrial Estates,
Selected Flats & Walkways, Stations and Selected Places of Interest.

HOW TO USE THIS INDEX

1. Each street name is followed by its Postcode District and then by its Locality abbreviation(s) and then by its map reference;
   e.g. **Abbotsford Rd.** CV11: Nun . . . .3A **32** is in the CV11 Postcode District and the Nuneaton Locality and is to be found in square 3A on page **32**. The page number is shown in bold type.

2. A strict alphabetical order is followed in which Av., Rd., St., etc. (though abbreviated) are read in full and as part of the street name;
   e.g. **Alder Ct.** appears after **Alderbrooke Dr.** but before **Alderman Gee Hall.**

3. Streets and a selection of flats and walkways too small to be shown on the maps, appear in the index with the thoroughfare to which it is connected shown in brackets; e.g. **Alderman Gee Hall** CV12: Bed . . . . .1E **35** (off Dempster Rd.)

4. Addresses that are in more than one part are referred to as not continuous.

5. Places and areas are shown in the index in **BLUE TYPE** and the map reference is to the actual map square in which the town centre or area is located and not to the place name shown on the map; e.g. **ANSLEY** 5B **20**

6. An example of a selected place of interest is Atherstone Arts Cen. 5D **4**

7. An example of a station is **Atherstone Station (Rail)** 5C **4**

8. An example of a hospital or hospice is BRAMCOTE HOSPITAL 4G **33**

GENERAL ABBREVIATIONS

Arc. : Arcade	**Dpt.** : Depot	**Lit.** : Little	**Rd.** : Road
Av. : Avenue	**Dr.** : Drive	**Lwr.** : Lower	**Shop.** : Shopping
Bri. : Bridge	**E.** : East	**Mnr.** : Manor	**Sth.** : South
Bldgs. : Buildings	**Ent.** : Enterprise	**Mkt.** : Market	**Sq.** : Square
Bus. : Business	**Est.** : Estate	**Mdw.** : Meadow	**St.** : Street
Cvn. : Caravan	**Fld.** : Field	**Mdws.** : Meadows	**Ter.** : Terrace
Cen. : Centre	**Flds.** : Fields	**M.** : Mews	**Trad.** : Trading
Chu. : Church	**Gdns.** : Gardens	**Mt.** : Mount	**Up.** : Upper
Circ. : Circle	**Gth.** : Garth	**Mus.** : Museum	**Vw.** : View
Cl. : Close	**Ga.** : Gate	**Nth.** : North	**Vis.** : Visitors
Comn. : Common	**Grn.** : Green	**Pde.** : Parade	**Wlk.** : Walk
Cnr. : Corner	**Gro.** : Grove	**Pk.** : Park	**W.** : West
Cotts. : Cottages	**Ho.** : House	**Pas.** : Passage	**Yd.** : Yard
Ct. : Court	**Ind.** : Industrial	**Pl.** : Place	
Cres. : Crescent	**Info.** : Information	**Pct.** : Precinct	
Cft. : Croft	**La.** : Lane	**Ri.** : Rise	

LOCALITY ABBREVIATIONS

Ald G : **Alderman's Green**	Bulk : **Bulkington**	High H : **Higham-on-the-Hill**	Stap : **Stapleton**
Ansl : **Ansley**	Burb : **Burbage**	Hinc : **Hinckley**	Stoke G : **Stoke Golding**
Ans C : **Ansley Common**	Burt H : **Burton Hastings**	K Mal : **Kirkby Mallory**	S Stan : **Stoney Stanton**
Arb : **Arbury**	Cald : **Caldecote**	Longf : **Longford**	S Chen : **Sutton Cheney**
Ash G : **Ash Green**	Dad : **Dadlington**	Man : **Mancetter**	Thurl : **Thurlaston**
Ash C : **Ashley Common**	Earl S : **Earl Shilton**	Nun : **Nuneaton**	Upton : **Upton**
Asty : **Astley**	Elme : **Elmesthorpe**	Pin : **Pinwall**	Whitt : **Whittington**
Aston F : **Aston Flamville**	Exh : **Exhall**	Rat C : **Ratcliffe Culey**	Wig P : **Wigston Parva**
Ath : **Atherstone**	Fen D : **Fenny Drayton**	Ridge L : **Ridge Lane**	With : **Witherley**
Barn : **Barnacle**	Gall C : **Galley Common**	Sap : **Sapcote**	Wlvy : **Wolvey**
Barw : **Barwell**	Gren : **Grendon**	Sharn : **Sharnford**	Wykin : **Wykin**
Bed : **Bedworth**	Griff : **Griff**	S Mag : **Sheepy Magna**	
Bram : **Bramcote**	Harts : **Hartshill**	Shil : **Shilton**	

A

	Adelaide Ct. CV12: Bed 3E **35**	Alec Wilson Sports Cen. 1F **35**	Ambleside LE9: Barw 6A **8**
	Admirals Way CV11: Bram . .5G **33**	Alesworth Dr. LE10: Burb 5F **27**	Ambleside Rd.
Abbey Ga. CV11: Nun 5G **23**	Adrian Dr. LE9: Barw 6G **7**	Alexander Av. LE9: Earl S 5D **8**	CV12: Bed 3E **35**
Abbey Ga. Shop. Pct.	Adrians' Cl. CV9: Man 1F **11**	Alexander Gdns.	Ambleside Way
CV11: Nun 5G **23**	Aintree Cl. CV12: Bed 1F **35**	LE10: Hinc 5C **16**	CV11: Nun 3A **24**
Abbey Grn. CV11: Nun 4F **23**	Alan Bray Cl. LE10: Hinc . . .2F **25**	Alexander Rd. CV12: Bed . . .2G **35**	Amelia Cl. CV12: Bulk 2E **37**
Abbey Sports Cen. 5F **23**	Alandale Ct. CV12: Bed 5A **34**	Alexandra Ct. CV9: Ath 5E **5**	Amos Av. CV10: Nun 1F **31**
Abbey St. CV11: Nun 4F **23**	Albert Rd. LE10: Hinc 6D **16**	Alexandra St. CV11: Nun . . .5F **23**	Amos-Jaques Rd.
(not continuous)	Albert St. CV10: Nun 6C **22**	Alfreton Cl. LE10: Burb 4F **27**	CV12: Bed 1E **35**
Abbotsbury Way	Albion Ct. CV11: Nun 6H **23**	Alice Cl. CV12: Bed 4D **34**	Anderton Rd. CV12: Bed 4A **34**
CV11: Nun 4B **32**	**Albrighton Wlk.**	Alliance Cl. CV11: Nun 6B **24**	Andrew Cl. CV13: Stoke G . . .2F **15**
Abbotsford Rd.	CV11: Nun 1C **32**	All Saints Cl. LE9: Sap 2H **29**	Angus Rd. LE9: Barw 1G **17**
CV11: Nun 3A **32**	**Alderbrooke Dr.**	**All Saints Rd.**	Anker Cl. CV11: Nun 6B **24**
Abbotts Grn. LE10: Burb 4F **27**	CV11: Nun 2C **32**	CV12: Bed 4D **34**	Anker St. CV11: Nun 6H **23**
Abeles Way CV9: Ath 3C **4**	Alder Ct. CV9: Ath 4D **4**	All Saints Sq. CV12: Bed . . .2F **35**	**ANSLEY** 5B **20**
Aberdeen Rd. CV11: Nun . . .2A **32**	**Alderman Gee Hall**	Alma Cl. CV11: Bram 5H **33**	**ANSLEY COMMON** 1E **21**
Abingdon Way CV11: Nun . . .2B **24**	CV12: Bed 1E **35**	Alma Rd. LE10: Hinc 6D **16**	Ansley Comn.
Acacia Cres. CV12: Bed . . .2H **35**	(off Dempster Rd.)	Almeys La. LE9: Earl S 5D **8**	CV10: Ans C 1E **21**
Acacia Rd. CV10: Nun 4C **22**	Alderney Cl. CV11: Bram . . .5H **33**	Almond Av. CV10: Nun 3A **22**	Ansley La. CV10: Ansl 6A **20**
Achurch Cl. LE9: S Stan . . .4H **19**	Alders, The CV12: Bed 3C **34**	Almond Way LE9: Earl S 1C **18**	Ansley Rd. CV10: Nun 6C **20**
Acorn Cl. CV12: Bed 5A **34**	Aldersgate CV11: Nun 6G **23**	Almshouses CV12: Bed 2G **35**	Ansley Rd. LE10: Burb 3C **26**
Adcote Cl. LE9: Barw 1G **17**	Alders La. CV10: Nun 2G **21**	Amberley Av. CV12: Bulk . . .2E **37**	Applebees Mdw.
Addison Cl. CV10: Gall C 4G **21**	Aldin Way LE10: Hinc 4A **16**	Ambien Rd. CV9: Ath 6D **4**	LE10: Hinc 3G **25**
	Aldridge Rd. LE10: Burb 3D **26**	Ambion Way LE10: Hinc 6F **17**	Appleby Ho. LE10: Hinc 6E **17**

B

Brisbane Ct. CV12: Bed 3E 35
Britannia Rd. LE10: Burb 4G 27
Britannia Shop. Cen.
   LE10: Hinc 6D 16
Britten Cl. CV11: Nun 4C 32
Brixham Cl. CV11: Nun 4B 24
Broadsword Way
   LE10: Burb 5D 26
Brockey Cl. LE9: Barw 6H 7
Brockhurst Av. LE10: Burb . .5D 26
Brodick Cl. LE10: Hinc 1A 26
Brodick Rd. LE10: Hinc 1H 25
Brodick Way CV10: Nun 6D 22
Bronte Cl. CV10: Gall C 4F 21
Bronze Cl. CV11: Nun 3A 32
Brookdale LE10: Hinc 1B 26
Brookdale Rd. CV10: Nun . . .2H 23
Brookes's Yard LE10: Hinc . . .6D 16
             (off King St.)
Brookfield LE10: Sharn 4G 29
Brookfield Rd. LE10: Burb . .3C 26
Brook La. CV10: Nun 3G 23
Brooklea CV12: Bed 3D 34
Brookside LE10: Burb 3D 26
Brook St. CV12: Bed 6F 31
Brook Wlk. CV9: Man 1F 11
Broomfield Ri. CV10: Nun . . .1D 30
Brosdale Dr. LE10: Hinc 6A 16
Broughton Rd. LE9: S Stan . .5H 19
Browning Cl. CV10: Gall C . .4G 21
Browning Dr. LE10: Hinc 6C 16
Brown's Cl. LE9: Sap 1H 29
Bruce Rd. CV7: Exh 6D 34
Brunel Rd. LE10: Hinc 1C 26
Bryant Rd. CV7: Exh 6E 35
Bryony Cl. CV12: Bed 4C 34
Buchan Cl. CV10: Gall C 5F 21
Buckingham Cl.
   CV10: Nun 2F 31
   LE10: Hinc 3E 17
Buckinghams Way
   LE10: Sharn 5F 29
Bucks Hill CV10: Nun 2H 21
Buckwell Rd. LE9: Sap 1H 29
BULKINGTON
   Bedworth 3E 37
Bulkington La. CV12: Bed . . .3C 32
Bulkington Rd. CV7: Shil . . .6G 37
   CV12: Bed 3G 35
Bullfurlong La. LE10: Burb . .4F 27
Bull Ring CV10: Nun 1F 31
Bull St. CV11: Nun 1H 31
Bumble Bee Gdns.
   LE10: Sharn 5G 29
BURBAGE 4G 27
Burbage Common Country Pk.
             . . . . .4H 17
Burbage Common Country Pk.
   Vis. Cen. 4H 17
Burbage Comn. Rd.
   LE9: Elme 4H 17
Burbage Rd. LE10: Hinc 1F 27
Burbage Wood Country Pk.
             . . . . .6H 17
Burbury Cl. LE10: Hinc 1G 35
Burgage Pl. CV11: Nun 5G 23
Burgage Wlk. CV11: Nun . . .4F 23
             (Friary St.)
   CV11: Nun 5G 23
            (Powell Way)
Burghley Cl. CV11: Nun 1B 32
Burleigh Rd. LE10: Hinc 5C 16
Burlington Rd. CV10: Nun . . .4F 31
Burnaby Cl. CV10: Nun 4H 21
Burnham Ri. CV11: Nun 3C 24
Burns Wlk. CV12: Bed 4G 35
Burnsway LE10: Hinc 6C 16
BURTON HASTINGS 3H 33
Burton La. LE9: Burt H 5H 33
Bute Cl. LE10: Hinc 6C 16
Butler's Cres. CV7: Exh 4E 35
Buttercup Way CV12: Bed . . .3B 34
Buttermere Av. CV11: Nun . .3C 24
Butt La. LE10: Hinc 6E 17
Butt La. Cl. LE10: Hinc 6E 17
Byford Cl. CV10: Nun 5D 22

Byford St. CV10: Nun 5D 22
Byron Av. CV12: Bed 3H 35
Byron St. LE9: Barw 5H 7
   LE9: Earl S 6C 8

C

Cadeby Cl. LE10: Hinc 5B 16
Cadles Cl. LE9: S Stan 3H 19
Cadman Cl. CV12: Bed 2G 35
Caernarvon Dr. CV11: Nun . .6H 23
CALDECOTE 5E 13
Caldecote Cl. CV10: Nun . . .2G 23
Caldecote Hall Dr.
   CV10: Cald 4D 12
Caldecote La. CV10: Cald . . .6D 12
Calder Cl. CV12: Bulk 3D 36
Caldon Cl. LE10: Hinc 1B 26
Caldwell Cvn. Pk.
   CV11: Nun 3H 31
Caldwell Ct. CV11: Nun 1H 31
Caldwell Rd. CV11: Nun 1G 31
Callendar Cl. CV11: Nun 2C 24
Calver Cres. LE9: Sap 2H 29
Camborne Dr. CV11: Nun . . .4B 24
Cambourne Rd.
   LE10: Burb 3G 27
Cambridge Dr. CV10: Nun . . .6C 22
Camelot M. LE10: Hinc 5B 16
Campbell Cl. CV10: Gall C . .5G 21
CAMP HILL 3B 22
Camp Hill Dr. CV10: Nun . . .2B 22
Camp Hill Rd. CV10: Nun . . .2H 21
Campling Cl. CV12: Bulk 3D 36
Campton Cl. LE10: Burb 2E 27
Canal Way LE10: Hinc 2H 25
Canberra Ct. CV12: Bed 3E 35
Canberra Way LE10: Burb . . .5E 27
Candle La. LE9: Earl S 5D 8
Canning St. LE10: Hinc 6C 16
Canterbury Way
   CV11: Nun 1C 24
Cardigan Rd. CV12: Bed 4A 34
Carey Hill Rd. LE9: S Stan . .5H 19
Carisbrook Rd. CV10: Nun . .3H 23
Carlton Cl. CV12: Bulk 2D 36
Carlyle Cl. CV10: Gall C 4F 21
Carlyon Rd. CV9: Ath 4E 5
Carlyon Rd. Ind. Est.
   CV9: Ath 4F 5
          (not continuous)
Carnoustie Cl. CV11: Nun . . .3E 33
Caroline Cl. CV11: Nun 4B 32
Carousel Pk. LE9: Barw 5F 7
Carpenters Cl. LE10: Burb . .4F 27
Carr's Dr. LE9: Earl S 5D 8
Carrs Hill LE9: Barw 1A 18
Carr's Rd. LE9: Earl S 5D 8
Cashmore Rd. CV12: Bed . . .4C 34
Castle Cl. LE9: Earl S 4D 8
   LE9: Sap 2H 29
Castle Ct. LE10: Burb 3D 26
Castlemaine Dr.
   LE10: Hinc 4E 17
Castle Rd. CV10: Harts 5H 11
   CV10: Nun 2G 23
Castle St. LE10: Hinc 1D 26
Castle Vw. Pk. Mobile Homes
   CV10: Harts 6H 11
Cavalier Cl. CV10: Nun 1A 32
Caversham Cl. CV11: Nun . .2B 24
Cecil Leonard Knox Cres.
   CV11: Bram 5H 33
Cedar Ct. LE10: Burb 3G 27
Cedar Rd. CV10: Nun 3B 22
   LE9: Earl S 6B 8
Cedars, The CV7: Exh 5E 35
Cedars Rd. CV7: Exh 4F 35
Celandine Way CV12: Bed . . .3C 34
Cemetery La. CV10: Harts . . .6H 11
Centenary Bus. Pk.
   CV10: Nun 6A 24
Central Av. CV11: Nun 4F 23
Centrovell Ind. Est.
   CV11: Nun 1G 31

Chalfont Cl. CV12: Bed 1E 35
Chamberlaine St.
   CV12: Bed 1F 35
Chancery Ct. CV10: Harts . . .2G 21
Chancery La. CV10: Harts . . .2H 21
Chandos St. CV11: Nun 5E 23
Change Brook Cl.
   CV11: Nun 1B 24
CHAPEL END 2H 21
Chapel La. CV9: With 5H 5
   LE10: Sharn 5G 29
Chapel St. CV11: Nun 5G 23
   CV12: Bed 2F 35
          (not continuous)
   LE9: Barw 1G 17
   LE9: Earl S 4E 9
   LE9: Stap 4F 7
   LE10: Sharn 5G 29
Chapel Yd. LE10: Hinc 1D 26
Charlecote Wlk.
   CV11: Nun 3B 32
Charles Eaton Rd.
   CV12: Bed 2D 34
Charles Rd. CV9: Man 6E 5
Charles St. CV11: Nun 4E 23
   LE10: Hinc 6E 17
Charleston Cres.
   LE9: Barw 1G 17
Charnwood Av. CV10: Nun . .1B 30
Charnwood Cl. LE10: Hinc . . .5E 17
Charnwood Dr.
   CV10: Harts 5G 11
Charnwood Rd. LE9: Barw . . .5H 7
   LE10: Hinc 5D 16
Chartwell Cl. CV11: Nun 2B 32
Chase Cl. CV11: Nun 3H 23
Chatsworth Cl. LE10: Burb . .3F 27
Chatsworth Dr. CV11: Nun . .1B 32
Chaucer Dr. CV10: Gall C . . .4G 21
Chaytor Dr. CV10: Nun 2G 21
Chelsea Cl. CV11: Nun 2B 24
Cheltenham Cl. CV12: Bed . .1F 35
Chequer St. CV12: Bulk 3E 37
Cherryfield Cl.
   CV10: Harts 5H 11
Cherry Orchard Est.
   CV13: High H 4B 14
Cherry Tree Av. CV10: Nun . .3C 22
Cherry Tree Dr. LE9: Barw . . .5H 7
Cherwell Cl. LE10: Hinc 1A 26
Chessher St. LE10: Hinc 6C 16
Chesterfield Way LE9: Barw . .6A 8
Chesterton Dr.
   CV10: Gall C 4F 21
Chestnut Cres. CV10: Nun . .3C 22
Chestnut Dr. CV11: Nun 6A 24
Chestnut Rd. CV12: Bed 1H 35
Chestnuts, The CV12: Bed . .3C 34
Chetwynd Dr. CV11: Nun 4D 32
Cheveral Rd. CV12: Bed 2E 35
Cheverel Pl. CV11: Nun 1F 31
Cheverel St. CV11: Nun 6F 23
Cheviot Cl. CV10: Nun 6H 21
Chichester Cl. CV11: Nun . . .2C 24
CHILVERS COTON 6F 23
Chilvers Cl. CV11: Nun 5G 23
Chilworth Cl. CV11: Nun 3A 32
Chines, The CV10: Nun 2H 23
   CV11: Nun 1H 31
Choyce Cl. CV9: Ath 3D 4
Christchurch Cl.
   CV10: Nun 2D 30
Church Cl. CV10: Harts 1H 21
   CV13: Stoke G 2F 15
   LE9: Barw 1G 17
   LE10: Burb 4G 27
Churchdale Cl. CV10: Nun . .5A 22
CHURCH END
   Nuneaton 3A 20
Chu. Farm Ct.
   LE10: Aston F 3C 28
Church La. CV7: Ash G 6C 34
   CV9: Rat C 1H 5
   CV10: Ansl 4A 20
   CV10: Nun 2G 23
   CV13: Fen D 1D 12

Church La. LE9: Barw 1G 17
   LE9: Stap 4E 7
Church Rd. CV9: With 5H 5
   CV10: Harts 1H 21
   CV10: Nun 6A 22
Church St. CV9: Ath 5D 4
   CV11: Nun 5G 23
   CV12: Bulk 3E 37
   LE9: Earl S 4D 8
   LE9: S Stan 5H 19
   LE9: Sap 2H 29
   LE10: Burb 3G 27
Church Wlk. CV9: Man, Ath . .5E 5
   CV11: Nun 1A 32
   CV12: Bed 3F 35
   LE9: Sap 2H 29
   LE10: Hinc 1D 26
Church Walks
   CV13: Stoke G 2F 15
Cicey La. CV11: Burt H 3H 33
Circle, The CV11: Nun 5C 22
Claremont Cl. CV12: Bulk . . .1D 36
Clarence Cl. LE10: Hinc 1E 27
Clarence Rd. LE10: Hinc 1E 27
Clarence St. CV11: Nun 5E 23
Clarendon Rd. LE10: Hinc . . .2C 26
Clarkes Yd. LE10: Hinc 6D 16
Clay Av. CV11: Nun 2A 24
Clear Vw. Cres. LE9: Earl S . .4D 8
Cleaver Gdns. CV10: Nun . . .3G 23
Clement St. CV11: Nun 6F 23
Clent Dr. CV10: Nun 6H 21
Cleveland Rd. CV12: Bulk . . .2D 36
   LE10: Hinc 1C 26
Cleveley Dr. CV10: Nun 2B 22
Clifton Cl. LE10: Hinc 6B 16
Clifton Rd. LE10: Hinc 5D 22
Clifton Way LE10: Hinc 5A 16
Clinic Dr. CV11: Nun 6G 23
Clint Hill Dr. LE9: S Stan 4H 19
Clinton Wlk. CV11: Nun 3A 32
Cloisters, The LE9: Earl S . . .5C 8
Close, The LE9: Barw 6H 7
   LE9: Stap 3F 7
   LE10: Sharn 5F 29
Closers Bus. Cen.
   CV11: Nun 1H 31
Clovelly Way CV11: Nun 4A 24
Clover Fld. LE10: Hinc 4C 16
Clover Pk. Trad. Est.
   LE10: Hinc 4B 16
Clunes Av. CV11: Nun 3A 24
Clyde Rd. CV12: Bulk 2C 36
COALPIT FIELD 3H 35
Coalpit Flds. Rd.
   CV12: Bed 3G 35
Colbek Ct. CV10: Gall C 5E 21
Coldstream Cl. LE10: Hinc . .6A 16
Coleshill Rd. CV10: Ans C . . .2C 20
   CV10: Harts 2G 21
Coleshill St. CV9: Ath 5D 4
Coley Cl. LE10: Hinc 2D 26
College La. LE10: Hinc 6E 17
College St. CV10: Nun 1F 31
Colliery La. CV7: Exh 4F 35
Colliery La. Nth. CV7: Exh . . .4F 35
COLLYCROFT 1F 35
Colts Cl. LE10: Burb 5D 26
Columbia Gdns.
   CV12: Bed 3H 35
Columbine Way
   CV12: Bed 4C 34
Common, The LE9: Barw 1H 17
Congreve Wlk. CV12: Bed . . .3F 35
Conifer Cl. CV12: Bed 1G 35
Conifer Ct. CV12: Bed 1G 35
Coniston Cl. CV12: Bulk 2E 37
   LE9: Earl S 5D 8
Coniston Cl. CV11: Nun 2B 24
   LE9: Earl S 5D 8
Coniston Way CV11: Nun . . .2B 24
Constable Cl. CV12: Bed 6E 31
Constance Cl. CV12: Bed . . .5D 34
Convent Cl. CV9: Ath 6F 5

Fisher Cl.—Higham La.

Fisher Cl. LE9: S Stan 5G **19**
Fishers Wlk. CV9: Ath 6D **4**
Fitton St. CV11: Nun 6F **23**
Five Foot LE10: Hinc 5D **16**
Flamville Rd. LE10: Burb 4H **27**
Fleet, The LE9: S Stan 3H **19**
Fleming Rd. LE10: Hinc 2G **25**
Fletcher Rd. LE9: S Stan 4H **19**
LE10: Burb 2E **27**
Flint Cl. CV9: Ath 3E **5**
Florence Cl. CV9: Ath 4D **4**
CV12: Bed 5D **34**
Florian Way LE10: Hinc 6H **15**
Flude Rd. CV7: Ash G 6A **34**
Ford St. CV10: Nun 5C **22**
Forest Rd. LE10: Hinc 1F **27**
Forest Vw. Rd. LE9: Barw 6H **7**
Forest Way CV10: Nun 1C **30**
Forresters Cl. LE10: Burb 3F **27**
Forresters Rd. LE10: Burb . . .3F **27**
Forryan Rd. LE10: Burb 2F **27**
Fosse Cl. LE10: Burb 4H **27**
LE10: Sharn 5F **29**
Fosse Meadows Nature Reserve 6G **29**
FOUR LANES END **4B 34**
Fourways Rd. CV9: Ath 5F **5**
Fox Av. CV10: Nun 1G **23**
Foxbank Ind. Est.
LE9: S Stan 4H **19**
Foxglove Cl. CV12: Bed 4C **34**
Foxhills Cl. CV11: Nun 2E **33**
Fox Hollies LE10: Sharn 5F **29**
Fox's Covert CV13: Fen D 1D **12**
Frances Cres. CV12: Bed 2E **35**
Frank Booton Cl.
LE9: Earl S 5F **9**
Franklin Ct. CV11: Nun 2H **31**
Franklin Rd. CV11: Nun 2H **31**
Frank St. CV11: Nun 6F **23**
Fraser Cl. CV10: Nun 3H **21**
Frederick Av. LE10: Hinc 5A **16**
Freeman Cl. CV10: Nun 5B **22**
Freemans La. LE10: Burb . . .4G **27**
Freer St. CV11: Nun 1A **32**
Freesland Ri. CV10: Nun 3H **21**
Frensham Dr. CV10: Nun 4H **21**
Freswick Cl. LE10: Hinc 6H **15**
Frewen Dr. LE9: Sap 1H **29**
Friar's Ga. CV9: Ath 5D **4**
Friary Cl. LE10: Hinc 6E **17**
Friary Rd. CV9: Ath 4D **4**
Friary St. CV11: Nun 4F **23**
Frisby Ct. CV11: Nun 1A **32**
Frisby Rd. LE9: Barw 6H **7**
Friswell La. LE9: Barw 6G **7**
Frith Way LE10: Hinc 4A **16**
Frobisher Cl.
LE10: Hinc 3D **16**
Frolesworth Rd.
LE10: Sharn 4H **29**
Furnace Cl. CV12: Bed 1H **35**
Furnace Rd. CV12: Bed 1H **35**

G

Gadsby Ct. CV11: Nun 6A **24**
Gadsby St. CV11: Nun 6H **23**
Gainsborough Av.
LE10: Hinc 4A **16**
Gainsborough Dr.
CV12: Bed 1E **35**
Gallagher Rd. CV12: Bed 3E **35**
GALLEY COMMON **4F 21**
Galloway Cl. LE9: Barw 1F **17**
Gallus Dr. LE10: Hinc 6A **16**
Gamecock Barracks
CV11: Bram 6H **33**
Garden Cl. LE10: Burb 3C **26**
Garden Gro. CV12: Bed 5D **34**
Garden Rd. LE10: Hinc 6D **16**
Garnette Cl. CV10: Nun 4H **21**
Garrett St. CV11: Nun 1A **32**
Gartree Cres. LE9: Earl S 5B **8**
Gatehouse La. CV12: Bed 3E **35**
George Eliot Av.
CV12: Bed 3H **35**
George Eliot Bldgs.
CV11: Nun 5G 23
(off Mill St.)
GEORGE ELIOT HOSPITAL . . .**1F 31**
George Eliot St.
CV11: Nun 1G **31**
George Foster Cl.
LE9: Earl S 4E **9**
George Fox La.
CV13: Fen D 1E **13**
George Geary Cl.
LE9: Barw 6A **8**
George Hill Cl.
LE9: S Stan 4H **19**
George Marriott Cl.
LE9: S Stan 6G **19**
George St. CV11: Nun 1A **32**
CV12: Bed 2F **35**
LE9: Barw 1H **17**
LE10: Hinc 1D **26**
George St. Ringway
CV12: Bed 2F **35**
George Ward Ct. LE9: Barw . . .6H **7**
Gibson Cres. CV12: Bed 4E **35**
Gilfil Rd. CV10: Nun 2F **31**
Gillett Cl. CV11: Nun 6F **23**
Gipsy La. CV10: Nun 5G **31**
CV11: Nun 5G **31**
Girtin Cl. CV12: Bed 1E **35**
Gladstone Cl. LE10: Hinc 4E **17**
Gladstone Ter. LE10: Hinc 1E **27**
Glebe Av. CV12: Bed 4C **34**
Glebe La. CV11: Nun 3B **24**
(not continuous)
Glebe Rd. CV11: Nun 5H **23**
LE10: Hinc 1F **27**
Glen Bank LE10: Hinc 6E **17**
Glenbarr Cl. LE10: Hinc 1A **26**
Glenbarr Dr. LE10: Hinc 1A **26**
Glendon Gdns. CV12: Bulk . . .2E **37**
Gleneagles Cl. CV11: Nun . . .2E **33**
LE10: Burb 5D **26**
Glenfield Av. CV10: Nun 2G **23**
Glenwood Gdns.
CV12: Bed 1E **35**
Gloucester Cl. CV11: Nun . . .2C **24**
Glovers Cl. CV9: Man 6F **5**
Glyn Cl. LE9: Barw 6G **7**
Gold Cl. CV11: Nun 3A **32**
Golf Dr. CV11: Nun 3C **32**
GOODYERS END **5A 34**
Goodyers End La.
CV12: Bed 5A **34**
Goosehills Rd. LE10: Burb . . .4E **27**
Goose La. LE9: Barw 2G **17**
Gopsall Rd. LE10: Hinc 5D **16**
Gordon Cl. CV12: Bed 1F **35**
Gorse Farm Rd. CV11: Nun . . .3D **32**
Gorsy Way CV10: Nun 4B **22**
Gosford Dr. LE10: Hinc 6A **16**
Gowrie Cl. LE10: Hinc 5B **16**
Grace Rd. LE9: Sap 1H **29**
Graham St. CV11: Nun 4G **23**
Gramer Ct. CV9: Man 1F **11**
Granby Cl. LE10: Hinc 2C **26**
Granby Rd. CV10: Nun 6D **22**
LE10: Hinc 2C **26**
Grand Dpt. Rd. CV11: Bram. . .5H **33**
Grange, The LE9: Earl S 6C **8**
Grange Cl. CV10: Nun 2A **22**
Grange Dr. LE10: Burb 4E **27**
Grange Rd. CV10: Harts 5H **11**
Grant Rd. CV7: Exh 5E **35**
Granville Gdns.
LE10: Hinc 1C **26**
Granville Rd. LE10: Hinc 1C **26**
Grasmere Cres. CV11: Nun . . .2B **24**
Grasmere Rd. CV12: Bed 3F **35**
Grassington Dr. CV11: Nun . . .1C **32**
Green, The CV9: Man 1G **11**
CV10: Harts 5H **11**
CV11: Nun 1A **32**
CV13: Dad 1G **15**
LE10: Sharn 5G **29**
Greencroft LE9: S Stan 6H **19**
Greendale Cl. CV9: Ath 6E **5**
Greendale Rd. CV9: Ath 6E **5**
Greenhill Dr. LE9: Barw 6H **7**
Greenhill Rd.
CV13: Stoke G 2F **15**
Green La. CV9: Gren 2A **4**
CV10: Nun 3A **22**
LE9: Earl S 4D **8**
LE9: Stap 3E **7**
Greenmoor Rd. CV10: Nun . . .5E **23**
LE10: Burb 4D **26**
Greenside Cl. CV11: Nun 2D **32**
Greens Yd. CV12: Bed 2F **35**
Greenway CV11: Nun 3D **32**
Greenwood Ct. CV11: Nun . . .6B **24**
Greenwood Rd.
CV13: Stoke G 2G **15**
Gresham Rd. CV10: Nun 3F **31**
GRIFF **5E 31**
Griff Cvn. Site CV10: Nun . . .4G **31**
GRIFF HOLLOW **3H 31**
Griff La. CV10: Griff 4D **30**
(not continuous)
Grosvenor Cres.
LE10: Burb 3G **27**
Grove, The CV12: Bed 2F **35**
LE10: Hinc 1C **26**
Grove Flds. CV10: Nun 1G **23**
Grovelands Ind. Est.
CV7: Exh 6E **35**
Grove Pk. LE10: Burb 3G **27**
Grove Pl. CV10: Nun 6B **22**
Grove Rd. CV9: Ath 6D **4**
CV10: Nun 6B **22**
LE10: Burb 4F **27**
Gwendoline Av. LE10: Hinc . . .5A **16**
Gypsy La. CV9: Ath 3D **4**
(not continuous)

H

Hadrian Cl. LE10: Hinc 6H **15**
Halberd Cl. LE10: Burb 5D **26**
Hallam Cl. LE9: Earl S 5E **9**
Hall Dr. CV13: Stoke G 2G **15**
Hall End CV11: Nun 1H **31**
Hall End Pl. CV11: Nun 1H **31**
Hall La. CV9: With 5H **5**
Hall Rd. LE10: Burb 3D **26**
Halls Ct. LE9: S Stan 5H **19**
Halls Cres. LE10: Sharn 4G **29**
(not continuous)
Hamilton Cl. CV10: Nun 5B **22**
CV12: Bed 4A **34**
LE10: Hinc 5A **16**
Hamilton Ct. CV10: Nun 5B **22**
Hamlet Cl. CV11: Nun 2C **32**
Hammersley St.
CV12: Bed 4C **34**
Hammond Bus. Pk.
CV11: Nun 6A **24**
Hammond Cl. CV11: Nun 6A **24**
Hampton Av. CV10: Nun 5H **21**
Hams Way LE10: Sharn 5F **29**
Hanbury Rd. CV12: Bed 1G **35**
Hangmans La. LE10: Hinc . . .4E **17**
Hanover Ct. LE10: Burb 3E **27**
Hanover Glebe CV11: Nun . . .1G **31**
Hansom Ct. LE10: Hinc 1D **26**
Hansom Rd. LE10: Hinc 5F **17**
Harcourt Gdns. CV11: Nun . . .6G **23**
Hardy Cl. CV10: Gall C 5G **21**
LE10: Hinc 3D **16**
Hare & Hounds La.
CV10: Nun 1E **31**
Harecroft Cres. LE9: Sap 1H **29**
Harefield La.
CV10: Nun, Arb 3C **30**
Harefield Rd. CV11: Nun 5G **23**
Harmony Ct. CV10: Nun 1F **31**
Harold St. CV11: Nun 6G **23**
Harper's La. CV9: Man 1G **11**
Harrington Way
CV10: Griff 4E **31**
Harrison Cl. LE9: Earl S 5D **8**
Harrison Cres. CV12: Bed 3E **35**
Harrowbrook Ind. Est.
LE10: Hinc 2G **25**
Harrowbrook Rd.
LE10: Hinc 2G **25**
Hartington Grn. LE10: Burb . .3E **27**
HARTSHILL **1G 21**
Hartshill Hayes Country Pk. 6G **11**
Hartshill Hayes Country Pk. Vis. Cen. 6F **11**
Harveys Cl. LE9: Sap 2H **29**
Harwood Dr. LE10: Hinc 3F **17**
Haselbury Cnr. CV10: Nun . . .2D **30**
Hastings Dr. LE9: Barw 6H **7**
Hathaway Dr. CV11: Nun 2C **32**
Hatters Ct. CV12: Bed 3G **35**
Hatters Dr. CV9: Ath 3D **4**
Haunchwood Pk. Dr.
CV10: Gall C 5E **21**
Haunchwood Pk. Ind. Est.
CV10: Gall C 5E **21**
Haunchwood Rd.
CV10: Nun 5B **22**
Hawk Cl. CV11: Nun 3D **32**
Hawkins Cl. LE10: Hinc 3D **16**
Hawley Rd. LE10: Hinc 2C **26**
Hawthorn Cres.
LE10: Burb 4E **27**
Hawthorne Ter. CV10: Nun . . .4C **22**
Hawthorne Way LE9: Barw . . .1H **17**
Hawthorn Way CV10: Harts . . .1G **21**
Hayes Grn. Rd. CV12: Bed . . .4D **34**
Hayes La. CV7: Exh 5D **34**
Hayes Rd. CV10: Harts 1G **21**
Hayle Cl. CV11: Nun 4C **24**
Hays La. LE10: Hinc 2B **26**
Hazel Cl. CV10: Harts 2G **21**
Hazel Gro. CV12: Bed 2H **35**
Hazell Way CV10: Nun 2E **31**
Hazell Way Ind. Est.
CV10: Nun 2E **31**
Hazel Rd. CV10: Nun 4B **22**
Hazel Way LE9: Barw 6G **7**
Heart of England Crematorium
CV11: Nun 6B **24**
Heart of England Way
CV11: Nun 6B **24**
Heath Av. CV12: Bed 4C **34**
Heath Ct. LE9: Earl S 6B **8**
HEATH END
Nuneaton **1D 30**
Heath End Rd. CV10: Nun . . .1C **30**
Heather Cl. CV10: Nun 6D **22**
Heather Ct. CV9: Ath 4D **4**
Heather Dr. CV12: Bed 3C **34**
Heath La. LE9: Barw 5A **8**
Heath La. Sth. LE9: Earl S 5B **8**
Heath Rd. CV12: Bed 4D **34**
Hebden Way CV11: Nun 1C **32**
Heckley Rd. CV7: Exh 6E **35**
Hedgerows, The CV10: Nun. . .3D **22**
Hedge Way CV10: Nun 2A **22**
Helena Cl. CV10: Nun 6D **22**
Helston Cl. CV11: Nun 4C **24**
Hemdale CV11: Nun 5C **24**
Hemsworth Dr. CV12: Bulk . . .3D **36**
Henley Cl. CV11: Nun 1B **24**
Henry St. CV11: Nun 1G **31**
LE10: Hinc 5A **16**
Henson Rd. CV12: Bed 4C **34**
Henson Way LE10: Sharn 4F **29**
Herald Way LE10: Burb 4D **26**
Herbert St. CV10: Nun 6C **22**
Hereford Cl. CV10: Nun 5C **22**
LE9: Barw 6F **7**
Hereford Rd. CV11: Bram 5H **33**
Herford Way LE10: Burb 3F **27**
Herons Ct. LE10: Hinc 2H **25**
Herring Rd. CV9: Ath 6E **5**
Hickman Rd. CV10: Gall C . . .5E **21**
Hidcote Cl. CV11: Nun 3B **32**
Higham La. CV11: Nun 4A **24**
CV13: Stoke G 3E **15**
LE10: Wykin 4G **15**

42 A-Z Nuneaton

Leyland Rd.—Newdigate Cl.

Leyland Rd. CV11: Nun 2A **32**
CV12: Bulk 3D **36**
Leysmill Cl. LE10: Hinc 6H **15**
Liberty Way CV11: Nun 6B **24**
Library Cl. LE10: Burb 4G **27**
Lichfield Cl. CV11: Nun 2C **24**
Lilac Cl. LE10: Burb 3E **27**
Lilac Rd. CV12: Bed 6H **31**
Lilleburn Dr. CV10: Nun 2G **21**
Lime Gro. CV10: Nun 4C **22**
LE9: Earl S 6C **8**
Limes, The CV12: Bed 3C **34**
Limes Coppice CV10: Ans C 2E **21**
Lincoln Av. CV10: Nun 2H **21**
Lincoln Rd. LE9: Barw 1G **17**
Linden Lea CV12: Bed 2F **35**
Linden Rd. LE10: Hinc 6C **16**
Lindley Rd. CV12: Bed 3B **34**
Lingwood Dr. CV10: Nun 6D **22**
Linwood Cl. LE10: Hinc 5B **16**
Liskeard Cl. CV11: Nun 4C **24**
Lismore Dr. LE10: Hinc 6B **16**
Lister Rd. CV9: Ath 4D **4**
Lister St. CV11: Nun 6H **23**
LITTLE BEDWORTH HEATH 4C **34**
Lit. Duke St. CV11: Nun 5F **23**
Livesey Ct. LE9: Sap 2G **29**
Livesey Dr. LE9: Sap 2G **29**
Lloyd Cl. CV11: Nun 1H **31**
Lobelia Cl. LE10: Burb 4E **27**
Lochmore Cl. LE10: Hinc 1A **26**
Lochmore Dr. LE10: Hinc 1A **26**
Lochmore Way LE10: Hinc 1A **26**
Lodge Cl. CV9: Man 1G **11**
LE10: Burb 4G **27**
Lomond Cl. LE10: Hinc 1B **26**
Lomond Way CV10: Nun 4A **22**
London Rd. LE10: Hinc 1E **27**
Longford Rd. CV7: Exh 6E **35**
Long Shoot, The CV11: Nun 4C **24**
Long St. CV9: Ath 5D **4**
CV12: Bulk 3F **37**
LE9: S Stan 4H **19**
Lossiemouth Rd.
LE10: Hinc 6H **15**
Loudon Ga. CV11: Nun 2B **32**
Lound Rd. LE9: Sap 1H **29**
Loveday Cl. CV9: Ath 3D **4**
Lovelace Cres. LE9: Elme 2D **18**
Love La. LE10: Burb 3G **27**
Lovell Cl. CV7: Exh 5E **35**
Lovell Rd. CV12: Bed 2E **35**
Lovetts Cl. LE10: Hinc 1H **25**
Lwr. Bond St. LE10: Hinc 6D **16**
Loweswater Cl. CV11: Nun 3C **24**
Lowry Cl. CV12: Bed 1E **35**
Lucas Rd. LE10: Burb 3D **26**
Lucas Way LE9: Earl S 6C **8**
Ludford Cl. CV10: Ansl 5B **20**
Ludford Rd. CV10: Nun 3A **22**
Lundy Cl. LE10: Hinc 6B **16**
Lupin Cl. LE10: Burb 3D **26**
Lutterworth Rd.
CV11: Bram, Burt H 5H **33**
CV11: Nun 1A **32**
LE10: Burb 4G **27**
Lutterworth Rd. Trad. Est.
LE10: Burb 4G **27**
Lychgate Cl. LE10: Burb 4G **27**
Lychgate La.
LE10: Aston F, Burb 4G **27**
Lydgate Ct. CV11: Nun 6G **23**
CV12: Bed 1E **35**
Lynch, The CV11: Nun 1H **31**
Lyndene Cl. LE9: Earl S 6D **8**
Lyndhurst Cl. LE10: Burb 3G **27**
Lyneham Cl. LE10: Hinc 6A **16**
Lynmouth Cl. CV11: Nun 4A **24**
Lysander Cl. LE10: Burb 5E **27**

M

McMahon Rd. CV12: Bed 5C **34**
Magee Cl. LE10: Hinc 5C **16**
Magyar Cres. CV11: Nun 4B **32**
Main Rd. CV9: Rat C 1G **5**
Main St. CV13: Dad 1G **15**
CV13: High H 4B **14**
CV13: Stoke G 2F **15**
LE9: Stap 4F **7**
LE10: Aston F 4C **28**
Maizefield LE10: Hinc 3C **16**
Malham Cl. CV11: Nun 1C **32**
Mallard Av. CV10: Nun 4A **22**
Mallard Dr. LE10: Hinc 2A **26**
Mallerin Cft. CV10: Nun 4H **21**
Mallory St. LE9: Earl S 5A **8**
Mallow Cft. CV12: Bed 3C **34**
Malthouse Cl. CV10: Ansl 5B **20**
Maltings, The CV11: Nun 4A **24**
Malt Mill Bank LE9: Barw 1G **17**
Malvern Av. CV10: Nun 6H **21**
MANCETTER 1G **11**
Mancetter Rd. CV9: Man 6F **5**
(not continuous)
CV10: Nun 2B **22**
Mandarin Cl. LE10: Hinc 3A **26**
Mnr. Brook Cl.
LE9: S Stan 4H **19**
Manor Cl. LE10: Burb 4C **26**
Manor Ct. Av. CV11: Nun 4F **23**
Manor Ct. Rd. CV11: Nun 5E **23**
Manor Cres. LE9: Stap 3E **7**
Manor Ho. Cl.
LE10: Aston F 3C **28**
Manor Pk. Rd. CV11: Nun 4E **23**
Manor Pl. LE10: Hinc 6D **16**
Manor Rd. CV9: Man 6E **5**
LE9: Sap 1H **29**
Manor Rd. Ind. Est.
CV9: Man 6E **5**
Manor St. LE10: Hinc 6C **16**
Manor Way LE10: Burb 4D **26**
Manse Cl. CV7: Exh 4E **35**
Mansion St. LE10: Hinc 6D **16**
Maple Av. CV7: Exh 4F **35**
Maple Cl. LE10: Burb 4E **27**
Maple Rd. CV10: Nun 4C **22**
Maples, The CV12: Bed 3C **34**
Maple Way LE9: Earl S 1B **18**
Marchant Rd. LE10: Hinc 1C **26**
Marchfont Cl. CV11: Nun 1C **32**
Margaret Av. CV12: Bed 2E **35**
Margaret Rd. CV9: Ath 6E **5**
Marie Cl. CV9: Man 6G **5**
Marigold Dr. LE10: Burb 4E **27**
MARKET END 3B **34**
Mkt. End Cl. CV12: Bed 4B **34**
Market Pl. *CV9: Ath* *5D* ***4***
(off Market St.)
CV11: Nun 5G **23**
LE10: Hinc 1D **26**
Market St. CV9: Ath 5D **4**
Marlborough Cl.
LE10: Burb 2H **27**
Marlborough Rd.
CV11: Nun 5F **23**
Marlowe Cl. CV10: Gall C 4F **21**
Marner Rd. CV10: Nun 2F **31**
CV12: Bed 2E **35**
Marriott Rd. CV12: Bed 3B **34**
Marsdale Dr. CV10: Nun 6C **22**
Marshall Rd. CV7: Exh 5D **34**
Marston Cl. LE9: S Stan 3H **19**
MARSTON JABBETT 6B **32**
Marston La. CV11: Nun 1A **32**
CV12: Bulk, Bed 1F **35**
Martin Cl. LE9: S Stan 6H **19**
Martindale Rd. CV7: Exh 5G **35**
Martins Dr. CV9: Ath 3D **4**
Martins Rd. CV12: Bed 4C **34**
Marwood Cl. CV11: Nun 4A **32**
MARY ANN EVANS HOSPICE 1E **31**
Maryland Cl. LE9: Barw 1F **17**
Mary St. LE9: Earl S 5D **8**
Marywell Cl. LE10: Hinc 6H **15**
Masefield Cl. LE9: Barw 5H **7**
Mason Ct. LE10: Hinc 1B **26**
Maughan St. LE9: Earl S 4D **8**
Mavor Dr. CV12: Bed 4B **34**
Mawnan Cl. CV7: Exh 5F **35**
Mayfair Dr. CV10: Gall C 5F **21**
Mayfield CV12: Bed 2F **35**
Mayfield Cl. CV12: Bed 2F **35**
Mayfield Rd. CV11: Nun 1A **32**
Mayfield Way LE9: Barw 6A **8**
Maynard Av. CV12: Bed 5B **34**
Mays Farm Dr. LE9: S Stan 4H **19**
Mays Farm Rd. LE9: S Stan 3H **19**
Meadow Cl. LE9: S Stan 4H **19**
Meadow Ct. CV11: Nun 4F **23**
Meadowcourt Rd.
LE9: Earl S 6D **8**
Meadow Dr. LE10: Burb 2G **27**
Meadow Rd. CV10: Harts 1G **21**
LE9: Barw 6A **8**
Meadows, The LE10: Burb 2G **27**
Meadowside CV11: Nun 2D **32**
Meadow St. CV9: Ath 6D **4**
CV11: Nun 4F **23**
Meadway, The LE10: Burb 2F **27**
Melbourne Cl. CV11: Nun 3A **32**
Melbourne Ct. CV12: Bed 3E **35**
Meldrum Rd. CV10: Nun 6B **22**
Melfort Cl. CV10: Nun 4A **22**
Melrose Av. CV12: Bed 5B **34**
Melrose Cl. LE10: Hinc 1B **26**
Melton St. LE9: Earl S 5C **8**
Melville Cl. CV7: Exh 5E **35**
Mendip Dr. CV10: Nun 6H **21**
Merevale Av. CV11: Nun 5E **23**
LE10: Hinc 2C **26**
Merevale Cl. LE10: Hinc 2C **26**
Merevale Ct. CV11: Nun 5E **23**
Merevale La. CV9: Ath 5A **4**
Merevale Rd. CV9: Ath 4C **4**
Merevale Vw. CV9: Ath 6C **4**
Merlin Av. CV10: Nun 3H **21**
Merrick Ct. LE10: Burb 4F **27**
Merrifield Gdns.
LE10: Burb 4E **27**
Merry Hurst Way
LE10: Hinc 2H **25**
Mersey Rd. CV12: Bulk 3C **36**
Metcalf Cl. LE9: S Stan 5H **19**
Metcalfe St. LE9: Earl S 6C **8**
Mews, The CV9: Ath 5E **5**
CV12: Bed 3F **35**
Middelburg Cl. CV11: Nun 2C **32**
MIDDLEFIELD 4C **16**
Middlefield Cl. LE10: Hinc 5D **16**
Middlefield Ct. LE10: Hinc 5D **16**
Middlefield La.
LE10: Hinc 4D **16**
(Middlefield Pl.)
LE10: Hinc 3C **16**
(Normandy Way)
Middlefield Pl. LE10: Hinc 4D **16**
Middlemarch Rd.
CV10: Nun 2F **31**
Middleton Cl. LE9: S Stan 5H **19**
Midland Rd. CV11: Nun 4E **23**
Milby Ct. CV11: Nun 1G **31**
Milby Dr. CV11: Nun 1B **24**
Mile Tree La. CV2: Ald G 6A **36**
Milfoil Cl. LE10: Hinc 2H **25**
Milford St. CV10: Nun 1F **31**
Millais Cl. CV12: Bed 1E **35**
Millais Rd. LE10: Hinc 4A **16**
Mill Cl. CV11: Nun 2B **32**
LE9: Sap 1H **29**
LE9: Stap 3E **7**
Millers Grn. LE10: Burb 3F **27**
Mill Farm Cvn. Pk.
CV12: Bulk 5D **32**
Mill Gdns. CV10: Nun 1F **31**
CV13: High H 4B **14**
Mill Hill Rd. LE10: Hinc 6C **16**
Milliners Ct. CV9: Ath 5D **4**
Mill La. CV9: Man 1G **11**
CV9: With 5G **5**
CV11: Burt H 3H **33**
CV12: Bulk 2C **36**
LE9: Earl S, Thurl 4E **9**
LE10: Sharn 4G **29**
Mill Race Vw. CV9: Ath 3D **4**
Mill St. CV11: Nun 5G **23**
CV12: Bed 2F **35**
LE9: Barw 2F **17**
Mill St. Ind. Est.
LE9: Barw 1G **17**
Mill Ter. CV12: Bed 6F **31**
Mill Vw. LE9: Stap 3F **7**
LE10: Hinc 6E **17**
Mill Wlk. CV11: Nun 5G **23**
Milner Cl. CV12: Bulk 3F **37**
Milton Cl. CV12: Bed 4H **35**
LE10: Hinc 6C **16**
Minions Cl. CV9: Ath 5D **4**
Mira Dr. CV10: Fen D 4G **13**
MIRAH HOUSE DAY HOSPITAL 4E **23**
Mistral Cl. LE10: Hinc 1F **27**
Mitchell Rd. CV12: Bed 3G **35**
Moat Farm Dr. CV12: Bed 5A **34**
Moat Gdns. LE9: Sap 2H **29**
Moat Way LE9: Barw 1F **17**
Mona St. LE9: Earl S 6C **8**
Monmouth Gdns.
CV10: Nun 6C **22**
Montana Wlk. CV10: Nun 6C **22**
Montgomery Rd.
LE9: Earl S 5E **9**
(not continuous)
Montrose Dr. CV10: Nun 6D **22**
Moorbrooke CV10: Harts 2G **21**
Moorcroft Cl. CV11: Nun 2D **32**
Moore Rd. LE9: Barw 5H **7**
Moorpark Cl. CV11: Nun 3E **33**
Moor Rd. CV10: Harts 1G **21**
Moorwood Cres.
CV10: Harts 1G **21**
Moorwood La. CV10: Harts 1F **21**
Moray Cl. LE10: Hinc 1A **26**
Morland Cl. CV12: Bulk 3F **37**
Morland Dr. LE10: Hinc 4B **16**
Morley Rd. LE9: Sap 2H **29**
Morris Dr. CV11: Nun 2H **31**
Mortiboys Way LE9: S Stan 5H **19**
Mossdale Cres. CV10: Nun 1D **30**
Mount Av. LE9: Barw 6A **8**
Mount Dr. CV12: Bed 2E **35**
Mountfield Rd. LE9: Earl S 5C **8**
MOUNT PLEASANT 2E **35**
Mount Pleasant Rd.
CV12: Bed 1E **35**
Mount Pleasant Ter.
CV10: Nun 3D **22**
Mount Rd. LE10: Hinc 1D **26**
Mount St. CV11: Nun 5F **23**
Mount St. Pas. CV11: Nun 5F **23**
Muirfield Cl. CV11: Nun 3E **33**
Mulberry Way CV10: Harts 1G **21**
Munnings Dr. LE10: Hinc 4A **16**
Myrtle Cl. LE9: Barw 6G **7**
Mythe La. CV9: With 3G **5**
Mythe Vw. CV9: Ath 4E **5**

N

Nairn Cl. CV10: Nun 1E **31**
Narrows, The LE10: Hinc 1E **27**
National Diving Cen. 6H **19**
Neale Cl. CV12: Bulk 4E **37**
Neales Ct. LE10: Hinc 6D **16**
Nelson Dr. LE10: Hinc 3D **16**
Netherley Ct. LE10: Hinc 4D **16**
Netherley Rd. LE10: Hinc 4D **16**
Netherwood Ind. Est.
CV9: Ath 4F **5**
Neville Smith Cl. LE9: Sap 2H **29**
New Bldgs. LE10: Hinc 6D **16**
New Century Way
CV11: Nun 5F **23**
Newcomen Cl. CV12: Bed 5B **34**
Newcomen Rd. CV12: Bed 4B **34**
New Cotts. CV10: Nun 6D **22**
Newdegate Pl. CV11: Nun 5G **23**
Newdegate St. CV11: Nun 5G **23**
Newdigate Cl. CV12: Bed 2E **35**

Newdigate Rd. CV12: Bed ...1E 35
Newey Av. CV12: Bed 5B 34
Newham Grn. CV10: Nun ...2A 22
Newland La. CV7: Ash G 6A 34
Newlands Rd. LE9: Barw 6H 7
Newlyn Cl. CV11: Nun 5B 24
Newman Cl. CV12: Bed 1F 35
Newquay Cl. CV11: Nun 4B 24
  LE10: Hinc 3E 17
New Rd. CV7: Ash G 6A 34
  CV9: Ath 6D 4
  LE9: S Stan 5H 19
  LE10: Burb 3G 27
Newstead Av. LE10: Burb ..5D 26
Newstead Cl. CV11: Nun ...1B 32
New St. CV12: Bed 3G 35
  CV12: Bulk 3E 37
  LE9: Earl S 5C 8
  LE9: S Stan 4H 19
  LE10: Hinc 6D 16
Newton Bldgs. CV12: Bed ...3F 35
Newton Cl. CV10: Harts 5H 11
Newton Rd. LE10: Hinc 2G 25
Newtown Rd. CV11: Nun 4G 23
  CV12: Bed 3D 34
  (not continuous)
New Wlk. LE9: Sap 2H 29
Nightingale Cl. CV9: Ath ...4E 5
Niton Rd. CV10: Nun 3H 23
Nock Verges LE9: Earl S 4E 9
  LE9: S Stan 5H 19
Nook, The CV11: Nun 1A 32
Norfolk Cl. LE10: Burb 5D 26
Norfolk Cres. CV10: Nun ...6C 22
Norman Av. CV11: Nun 5F 23
Norman Dagley Cl.
  LE9: Earl S 6C 8
Normandy Way LE9: Barw ..3E 17
  LE10: Hinc 6H 15
NORMANTON TURVILLE 3H 9
North Av. CV12: Bed 3H 35
Northbourne Dr. CV11: Nun .4A 32
North Cl. LE10: Burb 3E 27
Northcote Wlk. CV11: Nun ..3D 4
Northfield Rd. LE10: Hinc ..2B 26
Northleigh Way LE9: Earl S ..6D 8
North St. CV9: Ath 5D 4
Northumberland Av.
  CV10: Nun 5C 22
Norton Rd. LE9: Earl S 6A 8
Norwich Cl. CV11: Nun 1C 24
Norwood Cl. LE10: Hinc 4E 17
Notley Mnr. Dr. LE9: Barw ...5A 8
Nuffield Rd. LE10: Hinc 2G 25
NUNEATON 5G 23
Nuneaton Arts Cen. 5F 23
Nuneaton Borough FC 5D 22
Nuneaton La. CV13: High H. .5B 14
Nuneaton Mus. & Art Gallery
  ....5G 23
NUNEATON PRIVATE BMI
  HOSPITAL 2G 31
Nuneaton RFC 5B 24
Nuneaton Rd. CV9: Man ...1G 11
  CV10: Ansl 3A 20
  CV10: Harts 5H 11
  (Grange Rd.)
  CV10: Harts 4A 12
  (Woodford La.)
  CV12: Bed 6F 31
  CV12: Bulk 5D 32
Nuneaton Station
  CV10: Nun 4G 23
Nursery Gdns. LE9: Earl S ..6B 8
Nursery Rd. CV9: Ath 6F 5
  CV10: Ans C 1E 21
Nuthurst Cres. CV10: Ansl ..6C 20
Nuthurst La. CV10: Asty 6C 20
Nutt's La. LE10: Hinc 3H 25

O

Oak Cl. CV12: Bed 1G 35
  LE10: Burb 4E 27

Oakdale Rd. LE9: Earl S 6B 8
Oakdene Cres. CV10: Nun ..2G 23
Oak Dr. CV10: Harts 1G 21
Oakfield Gdns. CV9: Ath 6E 5
Oakham Cres. CV12: Bulk ..3F 37
Oakley Ct. CV12: Bed 4B 34
  (off Newcomen Rd.)
Oakroyd Cres. CV10: Nun ...2B 22
Oaks, The CV12: Bed 3D 34
Oaks Ind. Est. LE9: Earl S ..5C 8
Oaks Way LE9: Earl S 5C 8
Oaston Rd. CV11: Nun 5H 23
Oban Dr. CV10: Nun 1E 31
Oban Rd. LE10: Hinc 2A 26
Oberon Cl. CV11: Nun 2C 32
Occupation Rd.
  LE9: S Stan 2H 19
Odeon Cinema 5E 31
Odstone Dr. LE10: Hinc 1H 25
Okeford Way CV10: Nun ...2E 31
Oldany Way CV10: Nun 1D 30
OLDBURY 5E 11
Oldbury Rd. CV10: Harts ...6C 10
Oldbury Vw. CV10: Harts ...6H 11
Old Farm Rd. CV9: Man 1F 11
Old Forge Rd.
  CV13: Fen D 1E 13
Old Hinckley Rd.
  CV10: Nun 4H 23
Old Holly La. CV9: Ath 3C 4
Old Meeting Yd.
  CV12: Bed 2F 35
Old Watling St. CV9: Ath 5C 4
  (off Long St.)
Olton Cl. CV11: Burt H 3H 33
Olton Pl. CV11: Nun 5D 22
Orchard, The LE9: S Stan ..5H 19
Orchard Cl. CV9: With 5H 5
  CV10: Harts 2G 21
  LE10: Hinc 4G 27
Orchard Cotts. CV9: Ath 6E 5
Orchard Ct. CV9: Ath 6D 4
Orchard St. CV11: Nun 5H 23
  CV12: Bed 6F 31
  LE10: Hinc 1E 27
Orchid Cl. CV12: Bed 3C 34
Orford Ri. CV10: Gall C 5E 21
Orkney Cl. CV10: Nun 1D 30
  LE10: Hinc 6B 16
Ormes La. CV9: Rat C 1H 5
Ormond Cl. LE9: Barw 6G 7
Orton Rd. LE9: Earl S 5D 8
Orwell Cl. CV10: Gall C 4G 21
Osbaston Cl. LE10: Hinc 4F 17
Osprey Cl. CV11: Nun 3D 32
Outlands Dr. LE10: Hinc 6H 15
Outwoods, The LE10: Burb .1F 27
Outwoods Cl. CV9: Ath 6C 4
Oval, The LE9: S Stan 5H 19
Overbrook Grange
  CV11: Nun 6C 14
Owen Sq. CV9: Ath 5D 4
  (off Owen St.)
Owen St. CV9: Ath 5D 4
Oxford Cl. CV11: Nun 1B 24
Oxford St. LE9: Barw 6H 7
  LE9: Earl S 5D 8

P

Packwood Cl. CV11: Nun ...3B 32
Paddiford Pl. CV10: Nun ...6A 22
Paddock La. LE10: Burb 4F 27
Paddocks, The CV12: Bulk ..2D 36
Paddock Way LE10: Hinc ...2G 25
Padstow Cl. CV11: Nun 4B 24
Pallett Dr. CV11: Nun 2B 24
Palmer Rd. LE10: Hinc 5B 16
Pangbourne Cl.
  CV11: Nun 1B 24
Parade, The CV11: Nun 6G 23
Paragon Way CV7: Exh 5F 35
Park Av. CV11: Nun 6A 24
Park Cl. LE9: Earl S 4C 8

Park Ho. Ct. LE9: Sap 2H 29
Parkinson Dr. CV9: Ath 3E 5
Park La. CV10: Nun, Gall C ..5F 21
Park Rd. CV12: Bed 3F 35
  LE9: Earl S 5C 8
  LE9: Sap 2H 29
  LE10: Hinc 1E 27
Parkside Cl. LE10: Hinc 1E 27
Park St. CV11: Nun 6H 23
Park Vw. LE10: Sharn 4F 29
Park Vw. CV7: Exh 5E 35
Park Vw. Ct. CV10: Nun 5B 22
Parsons La. LE10: Hinc 1F 27
  LE10: Sharn 5G 29
Pavilions, The CV9: Ath 3C 4
Peacehaven Cotts.
  CV10: Nun 1E 31
Peake Av. CV10: Nun 1A 24
Pear Tree Av. CV10: Nun ...3C 22
Pear Tree Cl. LE9: Barw 5H 7
Pebblebrook Way
  CV12: Bed 4G 35
Peckleton Grn. LE9: Barw ..5H 7
Peggs Cl. LE9: Earl S 5D 8
Pembroke Cl. CV12: Bed ...4A 34
Pembroke Way CV11: Nun ..6H 23
Penfold Cl. LE9: Sap 1H 29
Pennant Rd. LE10: Burb 4D 26
Pennine Way CV10: Nun ...5H 21
Penny Hapenny Ct.
  CV9: Ath 5C 4
Penny La. LE9: Barw 6G 7
Penryn Cl. CV11: Nun 5C 24
Penshurst Way CV11: Nun ..3B 32
Pentire Cl. CV11: Nun 4B 24
Pentland Cl. LE10: Hinc 6B 16
Penzance Cl. LE10: Hinc ...3E 17
Penzance Way CV11: Nun ..4B 24
Peter's Cl. LE9: S Stan 5G 19
Pheasant Cl. CV12: Bed 4B 34
Phillip Docker Ct.
  CV12: Bulk 3D 36
Phoenix Bus. Pk.
  LE10: Hinc 1G 25
Phoenix Pk. CV7: Exh 6F 35
Phoenix Way CV7: Ash G ...6C 34
Pickford Cl. CV11: Nun 2C 32
Pike Cl. LE10: Burb 4D 26
Pilgrims Ga. LE10: Burb 4G 27
Pine Cl. CV13: Stoke G 2G 15
Pines, The CV12: Bed 3C 34
Pine Tree Cl. CV12: Bed ...1G 35
Pine Tree Rd. CV12: Bed ...1G 35
Pinfold Cl. LE10: Hinc 2H 25
Pingle Ct. CV11: Nun 1H 31
Pingles Leisure Cen. 1H 31
Pingles Stadium, The 1G 31
Pinwall La. CV9: Pin, Rat C ..1E 5
Pioneer Units CV11: Nun ...6A 24
Pipers La. CV10: Ans C 1C 20
Plough Hill Rd.
  CV10: Gall C, Ash C ...4F 21
Pool Bank St. CV11: Nun ...5F 23
Pool Rd. CV10: Nun 4D 22
Pool Rd. Bus. Cen.
  CV10: Nun 4D 22
Pool Rd. Ind. Est.
  CV10: Nun 4D 22
Poor's Piece Nature Reserve
  ....2B 22
Poplar Av. CV12: Bed 3H 35
Poplar Ho. CV12: Bed 3H 35
Poplars, The CV10: Nun 6B 22
  LE9: Earl S 4E 9
Poplar Way CV10: Harts ...2G 21
Portia Cl. CV11: Nun 2C 32
Portland Dr. CV10: Nun 5H 21
  LE10: Hinc 4E 17
Portreath Dr. CV11: Nun ...4C 24
Post Office La.
  CV9: With 6H 5
Potters Marston La.
  LE9: Thurl 5H 9
Potters Rd. CV12: Bed 4C 34
Pougher Cl. LE9: Sap 2H 29
Powell Way CV11: Nun 5G 23

Powers Rd. LE9: Barw 2F 17
Poyser Rd. CV10: Nun 3G 31
Praetor Ho. LE10: Hinc 6D 16
Prescelly Cl. CV10: Nun 6H 21
Preston Rd. LE10: Hinc 5B 16
Priesthills Rd. LE10: Hinc ..1D 26
Primrose Dr. CV12: Bed ...4C 34
  LE10: Burb 4E 27
Princes Av. CV11: Nun 6F 23
Princess Rd. CV9: Ath 4E 5
  LE10: Hinc 1E 27
Princes St. CV11: Nun 6F 23
Priors, The CV12: Bed 3G 35
Priory Ct. CV11: Nun 5E 23
  (not continuous)
Priory St. CV10: Nun 6A 22
Priory Wlk. CV9: Man 1F 11
  LE10: Hinc 6E 17
Private Rd. LE9: S Stan 4H 19
Prospect Way LE9: Earl S ..5C 8
Ptarmigan Pl. CV11: Nun ..6B 24
Pughe's Cl. LE10: Burb 4G 27
Purcell Av. CV10: Nun 4C 32
Purley Chase La.
  CV9: Man 5B 10
Purley Vw. CV9: Man 1F 11
Pyeharps Rd. LE10: Burb ...4E 27

Q

Quadrant, The CV11: Nun ..6A 24
Quaker Cl. CV13: Fen D 1E 13
Quantock Dr. CV10: Nun ...6H 21
Quarry La. CV9: Man 2E 11
  CV11: Nun 2B 32
Quarry Yd. CV10: Nun 5A 22
Queen Elizabeth Rd.
  CV10: Nun 3A 22
Queen Mary's Rd.
  CV12: Bed 6G 31
Queens Arc. CV11: Nun 5G 23
Queens Ct. CV11: Nun 5E 23
Queen's Pk. Flats
  LE10: Hinc 1E 27
  (off Queen's Rd.)
Queens Pk. Ter.
  LE10: Hinc 1E 27
Queens Rd. CV9: Ath 5E 5
  CV11: Nun 1E 27
Queen St. CV12: Bed 3G 35
  LE9: Barw 1H 17
Queensway CV10: Nun 3H 23
  LE9: Barw 6H 7

R

Rabbit La. CV12: Bed 1A 34
Racemeadow Rd. CV9: Ath ..4E 5
Radford Cl. CV9: Ath 3E 5
Radley Dr. CV10: Nun 2E 31
Radmore Rd. LE10: Hinc ...4D 16
Radnor Dr. CV10: Nun 1B 30
Raglan Cl. CV11: Nun 6H 23
Ragley Way CV11: Nun 1B 32
Railway Ter. CV12: Bed 3G 35
Rainsbrook Dr.
  CV11: Nun 2B 32
Raison Av. CV11: Nun 1B 24
Raleigh Cl. CV11: Nun 1B 24
Ramsden Av. CV10: Nun ...2A 22
Ramsden Rd. CV9: Man 6G 5
Ramsey Cl. LE10: Hinc 6B 16
Randle Rd. CV10: Nun 5B 22
Rannoch Cl. LE10: Hinc 1B 26
Rannoch Dr. CV10: Nun ...4A 22
Ratcliffe Ct. CV10: Nun 5A 22
RATCLIFFE CULEY 1H 5
Ratcliffe La. CV9: S Mag ...1F 5
Ratcliffe Rd. CV9: Ath 5E 5
  LE10: Burb 3F 27
Ratcliffe St. CV9: Ath 5D 4
Raveloe Dr. CV11: Nun 2H 31
Raven Way CV11: Nun 1B 32

Rawn Vw.—Springfield Rd.

Rawn Vw. CV9: Man 1F **11**
Raynor Cres. CV12: Bed 4B **34**
Raywoods, The
CV10: Nun 6D **22**
Reading Av. CV11: Nun 1B **24**
Rectory Cl. CV7: Exh 4E **35**
Rectory Dr. CV7: Exh 4E **35**
Red Deeps CV11: Nun 3H **31**
Red Hall Dr. LE9: Barw 6H **7**
Red Hall Rd. LE9: Barw 6A **8**
Redruth Cl. CV11: Nun 5C **24**
Redwood Cft. CV10: Nun 1E **31**
Reeves Rd. LE10: Burb 3F **27**
Regal Ct. CV9: Ath 5E **5**
Regency Cl. CV10: Nun 3H **23**
Regency Ct. LE10: Burb 2G **27**
Regent Ct. LE10: Hinc 1D **26**
Regent Pde. *LE10: Hinc 1D 26*
(off Regent St.)
Regent St. CV11: Nun 4G **23**
CV12: Bed 1G **35**
LE9: Barw 6H **7**
LE10: Hinc 1D **26**
Reg Hadden Ct.
CV10: Nun 3H **23**
Renison Rd. CV12: Bed 4C **34**
Repington Av. CV9: Ath 3D **4**
Reuben Av. CV10: Nun 3H **21**
Reynolds Cl. LE10: Hinc 4A **16**
Reynolds Rd. CV12: Bed 1E **35**
Rhyl Rd. CV11: Bram 5H **33**
Ribble Cl. CV12: Bulk 3D **36**
Ribblesdale Av.
LE10: Hinc 4E **17**
Ribbonbrook CV11: Nun 6H **23**
Ribbonfields CV11: Nun 6H **23**
Richardson Cl.
LE9: S Stan 6H **19**
Richmond Rd. CV9: Ath 6D **4**
CV11: Nun 6E **23**
LE10: Hinc 4C **16**
Riddon Dr. LE10: Hinc 1B **26**
RIDGE LANE **5A 10**
Ridge La. CV10: Ridge L 5A **10**
Ridgeway, The LE10: Burb 3D **26**
Riley Cl. LE9: S Stan 6H **19**
Rills, The LE10: Hinc 5E **17**
River Cl. CV12: Bed 4D **34**
River Dr. CV9: Ath 3D **4**
Rivermead CV11: Nun 5E **23**
Riversdale Rd. CV9: Ath 5F **5**
Riverside CV9: With 6H **5**
Riversley Rd. CV11: Nun 6G **23**
Roadway Cl. CV12: Bed 3F **35**
Roanne Ringway
CV11: Nun 5F **23**
Robert Rd. CV7: Exh 5D **34**
Robertson Cl. LE9: S Stan 5H **19**
Robinson Rd. CV12: Bed 5B **34**
ROBINSON'S END **6G 21**
Robinson Way LE10: Burb 5F **27**
Robins Way CV10: Nun 6G **21**
Rochester Cl. CV11: Nun 6F **23**
Rock Cl. CV10: Gall C 5F **21**
Rockingham Dr.
CV11: Nun 4B **32**
Rodney Cl. LE10: Hinc 3D **16**
Rogue's La. LE10: Hinc 2A **16**
Roman Cl. LE9: Earl S 4E **9**
Romney Cl. LE10: Hinc 4A **16**
Romsey Av. CV10: Nun 1H **23**
Ronald Toon Rd.
LE9: Earl S 5E **9**
Rookery, The CV10: Gall C 4E **21**
CV10: Ridge L 5A **10**
Rookery Cl. CV13: Fen D 1E **13**
Rosehill CV9: Ath 6F **5**
Rose La. CV11: Nun 6G **23**
Rosemary Way LE10: Hinc 2B **26**
Rosemullion Cl. CV7: Exh 5F **35**
Roseway CV13: Stoke G 2F **15**
Rosewood CV11: Nun 2B **32**
Rose Wood Cl. LE10: Burb 3F **27**
Rossendale Rd. LE9: Earl S 5B **8**
Rossendale Way
CV10: Nun 1B **30**
Ross Way CV11: Nun 4D **32**
Roston Dr. LE10: Hinc 6H **15**
Rothesay Cl. CV10: Nun 1E **31**
Roundhills, The LE9: Elme 2D **18**
Rowan Cen., The CV9: Ath 5E **5**
Rowan Rd. CV10: Nun 3A **22**
Rowans, The CV12: Bed 3C **34**
Rowan Way CV10: Harts 1F **21**
Rowlands Way CV9: Ath 3C **4**
Roxburgh Rd. CV11: Nun 2A **32**
Royal Ct. LE10: Hinc 2D **26**
Royal Mdw. Dr. CV9: Ath 3E **5**
Royal Oak La. CV7: Ash G 6A **34**
CV12: Bed 6A **34**
Royal Oak Yd. CV12: Bed 1F **35**
Rufford Cl. LE10: Burb 6D **26**
Rugby Rd. CV12: Bulk 3F **37**
LE10: Hinc, Burb 1C **26**
Runnymede Gdns.
CV10: Nun 6D **22**
Ruskin Cl. CV10: Gall C 4G **21**
Rutherford Glen
CV11: Nun 2B **32**
Rutland Av. CV10: Nun 5D **22**
LE10: Hinc 2C **26**
Rydal Av. CV11: Nun 3C **24**
Rydal Cl. LE10: Hinc 2H **25**
Ryde Av. CV10: Nun 3H **23**
Ryders Hill Cres.
CV10: Nun 2A **22**
Rye Piece CV12: Bed 3G **35**
Rye Piece Ringway
CV12: Bed 2F **35**
Ryhope Cl. CV12: Bed 4A **34**
RYTON **3F 37**

S

Saddlers Cl. LE10: Burb 3F **27**
Sadler Gdns. CV12: Bed 3G **35**
Saffron Cl. LE9: Barw 5A **8**
Saffron Ct. LE9: Barw 1G **17**
St Agnes Way CV11: Nun 5A **24**
St Andrews Dr. CV11: Nun 2D **32**
St Austell Cl. CV11: Nun 4C **24**
St Benedicts Cl. CV9: Ath 5D **4**
St Buryan Cl. CV11: Nun 4C **24**
St Catherine's Cl.
LE10: Burb 2F **27**
St Davids Way CV10: Griff 5E **31**
St Francis Cl. LE10: Hinc 4C **16**
St George's Av. LE10: Hinc 6C **16**
St George's Rd. CV9: Ath 3D **4**
St Georges Way
CV10: Nun 2F **31**
St Giles Rd. CV7: Ash G 6B **34**
St Helen's Cl. LE10: Sharn 4G **29**
St Ives Way CV11: Nun 4B **24**
St James Gdns.
CV12: Bulk 3E **37**
St James's Cl. LE10: Burb 4D **26**
St Johns LE10: Hinc 6E **17**
St Johns Rd. CV10: Ans C 1E **21**
St Lawrence Rd.
CV10: Ansl 5B **20**
St Luke's Way CV10: Nun 5A **22**
St Margaret Rd.
CV13: Stoke G 2G **15**
St Mark's Cl. CV10: Nun 5A **22**
St Martins LE10: Burb 3D **26**
LE9: Stap 3E **7**
St Mary's Av. LE9: Barw 2F **17**
St Mary's Ct. *CV11: Nun 4F 23*
(off Abbey Grn.)
LE9: Barw 1G **17**
St Mary's Rd. CV9: Ath 5E **5**
CV11: Nun 4F **23**
LE10: Hinc 1D **26**
St Matthew's Cl.
CV10: Nun 5A **22**
St Michaels Cl. CV9: Ath 4E **5**
St Michaels Ct.
LE9: S Stan 5H **19**
St Michael's Way
CV10: Nun 5A **22**
ST NICOLAS PARK **2B 24**
St Nicolas Pk. Dr.
CV11: Nun 2A **24**
St Nicolas Rd. CV11: Nun 4H **23**
St Paul's Gdns. LE10: Hinc 6E **17**
St Paul's Rd. CV10: Nun 6A **22**
St Peter's Av. CV9: With 6H **5**
St Peter's Cl. CV9: With 6H **5**
St Peter's Dr. CV10: Gall C 5F **21**
St Peters Rd. CV9: Man 6G **5**
Saints Way CV10: Nun 4H **23**
St Thomas's Cl.
CV10: Nun 6A **22**
Salcombe Cl. CV11: Nun 4B **24**
Salem Rd. LE10: Burb 4F **27**
Salisbury Av. CV10: Nun 2H **21**
Salisbury Dr. CV10: Nun 2H **21**
Salisbury Rd. LE10: Burb 2G **27**
Sandby Cl. CV12: Bed 1E **35**
Sanders Cl. CV9: Ath 4E **5**
Sandford Cl. LE10: Hinc 6F **17**
Sandon Rd. CV11: Nun 4F **23**
Sandpits, The CV12: Bulk 3E **37**
Sandringham Av.
LE9: Earl S 6B **8**
Sandringham Ct.
CV10: Nun 3D **22**
Sandy Cres. LE10: Hinc 6B **16**
Sandy Wlk. LE10: Hinc 5A **16**
SAPCOTE **2H 29**
Sapcote Rd. LE9: S Stan 5H **19**
LE10: Burb 2G **27**
Saunders Av. CV12: Bed 3F **35**
Saville Cl. LE10: Hinc 4E **17**
School Cl. LE10: Burb 3G **27**
School Hill CV10: Harts 2G **21**
School La. CV7: Exh 6C **34**
CV10: Gall C 3E **21**
LE9: Stap 3E **7**
LE10: Sharn 5G **29**
School Rd. CV12: Bulk 3D **36**
School Wlk. CV11: Nun 6A **24**
Scott Av. CV10: Nun 1H **23**
Seaforth Dr. LE10: Hinc 6A **16**
Sealand Dr. CV12: Bed 2E **35**
Seaton Cl. CV11: Nun 4B **24**
LE10: Burb 2G **27**
Seeswood Cl. CV10: Nun 1A **30**
Selby Way CV10: Nun 4H **21**
Sennen Cl. CV11: Nun 4C **24**
Sephton Dr. CV6: Longf 6G **35**
Severn Av. LE10: Hinc 1A **26**
Severn Rd. CV12: Bulk 2C **36**
Seymour Rd. CV11: Nun 6H **23**
Shackleton Dr. LE10: Burb 5E **27**
Shadrack Cl. LE9: S Stan 6H **19**
Shakespeare Av.
CV12: Bed 3H **35**
Shakespeare Dr.
CV11: Nun 2C **32**
LE10: Hinc 6C **16**
Shanklin Dr. CV10: Nun 3H **23**
Sharnbrook Gdns.
LE10: Sharn 5G **29**
SHARNFORD **5G 29**
Sharnford Rd. LE9: Sap 2H **29**
LE10: Aston F 3C **28**
Sharpless Rd. LE10: Burb 2E **27**
Sharratt Rd. CV12: Bed 3D **34**
Shawe Av. CV10: Nun 2G **23**
Sheepy Cl. LE10: Hinc 6F **17**
Sheepy Rd. CV9: Ath 2D **4**
Shelley Cl. CV12: Bed 4H **35**
Shelley Gdns. LE10: Hinc 4E **17**
Shenton Cl.
CV13: Stoke G 2G **15**
Shenton La. CV13: Dad 1G **15**
Shenton Rd. LE9: Barw 6H **7**
Shepperton Bus. Pk.
CV11: Nun 2G **31**
Shepperton Ct. CV11: Nun 1G **31**
Shepperton St. CV11: Nun 1G **31**
Sherborne Rd. LE10: Burb 2H **27**
Sherbourne Av.
CV10: Nun 4H **21**
Sheridan Dr. CV10: Gall C 4F **21**
Sheringham Cl. CV11: Nun 1B **32**
Sherwood Rd.
CV13: Stoke G 2F **15**
Shetland Dr. CV10: Nun 1D **30**
Shillingstone Dr.
CV10: Nun 2D **30**
Shilton La. CV12: Bulk 4F **37**
Shilton La. Ind. Est.
CV7: Shil 6G **37**
Shilton Rd. LE9: Barw 1H **17**
LE9: K Mal 1B **8**
Shoesmith Cl. LE9: Barw 1G **17**
Short St. CV10: Nun 5A **22**
Shrewsbury Cl. LE9: Barw 6G **7**
Sidmouth Cl. CV11: Nun 4B **24**
Silken Ct. CV11: Nun 6F **23**
Silver Birch Av. CV12: Bed 3C **34**
Silverbirch Cl. CV10: Harts 2G **21**
Silver Trees Dr. CV12: Bulk 1D **36**
Silver Wlk. CV10: Nun 6D **22**
Simmonds Way CV9: Ath 3D **4**
Simon Cl. CV11: Nun 1H **31**
Simon Ct. CV7: Exh 5E **35**
Sinclair Dr. CV6: Longf 6G **35**
Sisley Way LE10: Hinc 4A **16**
Skelwith Ri. CV11: Nun 3C **24**
SKETCHLEY **4E 27**
Sketchley Hall Gdns.
LE10: Burb 4C **26**
SKETCHLEY HILL **3E 27**
Sketchley La. CV9: Rat C 1H **5**
LE10: Burb 4B **26**
Sketchley La. Ind. Est.
LE10: Burb 4B **26**
Sketchley Mnr. La.
LE10: Burb 4D **26**
Sketchley Mdws.
LE10: Burb 4C **26**
Sketchley Mdws. Bus. Pk.
LE10: Burb 4C **26**
Sketchley Old Village
LE10: Burb 4C **26**
Sketchley Rd. LE10: Burb 4E **27**
Skey Dr. CV10: Nun 3H **21**
Skye Cl. CV10: Nun 1D **30**
Slack's Av. CV9: Ath 6D **4**
Slade Cl. CV11: Nun 3E **33**
Sleath's Yd. CV12: Bed 2F **35**
Sleets Yd. CV12: Bed 3F **35**
Slingsby Cl. CV11: Nun 1A **32**
Smallman Rd. CV10: Nun 2G **21**
Smarts Rd. CV12: Bed 4D **34**
Smercote Cl. CV12: Bed 4B **34**
Smith St. CV12: Bed 4C **34**
Smithy Farm Dr.
LE9: S Stan 5G **19**
Smorrall La. CV12: Bed 3A **34**
Snowdon Cl. CV10: Nun 6H **21**
Snowdrop Cl. CV12: Bed 4C **34**
Snowshill Cl. CV11: Nun 3B **32**
Soar Way LE10: Hinc 1A **26**
Somerset Dr. CV10: Nun 5C **22**
Sorrell Pl. CV10: Nun 3H **31**
Sorrell Rd. CV10: Nun 2H **31**
South Dr. LE9: S Stan 6H **19**
Southfield Cl. CV10: Nun 4H **23**
Southfield Rd. LE10: Hinc 2D **26**
Southlands CV9: Ath 6E **5**
South St. CV9: Ath 5D **4**
Spa Cl. LE10: Hinc 6E **17**
Spa Dr. LE9: Sap 1H **29**
Spa La. LE10: Hinc 6E **17**
Spencer St. LE10: Hinc 6D **16**
Spindles, The LE10: Burb 4F **27**
Spinney, The CV9: Man 6G **5**
Spinney La. CV10: Nun 5A **22**
Spinney Rd. LE10: Burb 3C **26**
Spires, The CV10: Nun 5A **22**
Spitalfields CV12: Bed 3G **35**
Springdale Ct. CV11: Nun 6H **23**
SPRINGFIELD **4F 35**
Springfield Cres.
CV12: Bed 3F **35**
Springfield Pk. LE10: Hinc 4A **16**
Springfield Rd. CV11: Nun 1A **32**
LE10: Hinc 2D **26**

Spring Gdns. LE9: Earl S 4D 8
  LE9: Sap 1H 29
Springhill CV10: Harts 1G 21
Spring Hill Rd. CV10: Nun . . .3A 22
Spring Rd. CV7: Barn 6D 36
Square, The CV11: Nun 1A 32
  LE9: Earl S 5C 8
  LE9: Sap 2H 29
Squires Grn. LE10: Burb 3F 27
Stables, The LE10: Burb 4D 26
Stable Wlk. CV11: Nun 1B 32
Stafford CV12: Bulk 3E 37
Stafford St. CV9: Ath 6D 4
  LE9: Barw 1G 17
Staines Cl. CV11: Nun 2B 24
Stainforth Cl. CV11: Nun . . .1B 32
Stanley Rd. CV9: Ath 6D 4
  CV11: Nun 4E 23
  LE10: Hinc 5C 16
Stanley St. LE9: Barw 1G 17
Stanton La. LE9: Sap 1F 29
Stanton Rd. LE9: Elme 3E 19
  LE9: Sap 2H 29
Stan Williams Ct.
  CV11: Nun 5H 23
Staples Cl. CV12: Bulk 2E 37
STAPLETON 4F 7
Stapleton La. CV13: Dad . .1H 15
  LE9: Barw 4F 7
  LE9: K Mal, Stap 1E 7
Starley Rd. CV7: Exh 5F 35
Startin Cl. CV7: Exh 6D 34
Station Rd. CV13: High H . . .3B 14
  CV13: Stoke G 2E 15
  LE9: Earl S 1C 18
  LE9: Elme 2C 18
  LE10: Hinc 1D 26
Station St. CV9: Ath 5D 4
Station Yd. LE10: Hinc 5D 16
Stephenson Rd. CV7: Exh . .6G 35
  LE10: Hinc 2G 25
Steppey La. CV9: Man 3D 10
Sterling Way CV11: Nun 3A 32
Stevens Cl. LE9: S Stan 5H 19
Stewart St. CV11: Nun 6F 23
Stirling Av. LE10: Hinc 6A 16
STOCKINGFORD 6B 22
Stockwell Head LE10: Hinc . .6D 16
STOKE GOLDING 2F 15
Stoke La. CV13: Dad 1G 15
  CV13: High H, Stoke G
  . . . . .3C 14 & 3E 15
  LE10: Wykin 4H 15
Stoke Rd. CV13: Stoke G 2H 15
  LE10: Hinc 2A 16
Stokesay Cl. CV11: Nun 6E 23
Stoneleigh Cl.
  CV10: Harts 5H 11
Stoneleigh Ct. CV11: Nun . .6G 23
Stoneley Rd.
  CV13: Stoke G 3F 15
Stonewell Cres.
  CV11: Nun 3D 32
Stoneycroft Rd. LE9: Earl S . .6B 8
STONEYGATE 5E 17
Stoneygate Dr. LE10: Hinc . .4E 17
Stoney Rd. CV10: Nun 3E 23
STONEY STANTON 5H 19
Stratford Av. CV9: Ath 6C 4
Stratford St. CV11: Nun 5G 23
Strathmore Rd.
  LE10: Hinc 2A 26
Stratton St. CV9: Ath 5E 5
Stretton Cl. LE10: Burb 3D 26
Stretton Rd. CV10: Nun 6E 23
Stroma Way CV10: Nun 1D 30
Strutt Rd. LE10: Burb 4G 27
Stubbs Cl. CV12: Bed 1E 35
Sudeley Rd. CV10: Nun 3G 31
Suffolk Cl. CV10: Nun 6C 22
  CV12: Bed 2E 35
Sunart Way CV10: Nun 4A 22
Sunningdale Cl.
  CV11: Nun 2C 32
Sunnydale Cres.
  LE10: Hinc 2A 26

Sunnydale Rd. LE10: Hinc . . .2H 25
Sunnyhill LE10: Burb 2F 27
Sunnyhill Sth. LE10: Burb . . .3F 27
Sunnyside LE10: Hinc 4E 17
Sunnyside Ct. CV10: Nun . . .6D 22
Sunnyside Pk. LE10: Hinc . . .3D 16
Sunnyside Pk. Ind. Est.
  LE10: Hinc 3C 16
Surrey Cl. CV10: Nun 6C 22
  LE10: Burb 5E 27
Sussex Cl. CV10: Nun 6C 22
Sutherland Dr. CV12: Bed . . .1E 35
Sutton Cl. LE10: Hinc 4F 17
Sutton La.
  CV13: Dad . . . . . .2A 6 & 1G 15
Sutton Pk. CV10: Nun 2H 21
Swains Grn. LE10: Burb 3F 27
Swallow Ct. CV12: Bed 5A 34
Swinburne Cl. CV10: Gall C . .4G 21
Swinburne Rd. LE10: Hinc . .6C 16
Sword Dr. LE10: Hinc 4B 16
Sycamore Cl. LE10: Burb . . .4E 27
Sycamore Rd. CV10: Nun . . .3B 22
Sycamores, The
  CV12: Bed 3C 34
Sydney Ct. CV12: Bed 3E 35

Tamar Cl. CV12: Bulk 2D 36
Tamar Rd. CV12: Bulk 2D 36
Tame Way LE10: Hinc 1A 26
Tannery Cl. LE10: Hinc 5E 5
Tansey Cres. LE9: S Stan . . .5G 19
Tarn Cl. CV12: Bed 3E 35
Taverners La. CV9: Ath 6D 4
Tavistock Way CV11: Nun . . .4A 24
Taylor Cl. LE9: S Stan 5H 19
Tea Gdn., The CV12: Bed . . .5C 34
Teal Bus. Pk. LE10: Hinc 2G 25
Teal Dr. LE10: Hinc 3A 26
Teignbank Cl. LE10: Hinc . . .5D 16
Teignbank Rd. LE10: Hinc . . .4C 16
Telford Rd. CV7: Exh 5G 35
Templer Ct. CV11: Nun 6G 23
Tenby Cl. CV12: Bed 4A 34
Tenlons Rd. CV10: Nun 1D 30
Tenlons Rd. Ind. Est.
  CV10: Nun 1D 30
Tennant St. CV11: Nun 6A 24
Tennyson Rd. LE10: Hinc . . .6B 16
Tenter St. CV9: Ath 5D 4
Terrace Rd. CV9: Ath 5D 4
Tewkesbury Dr. CV12: Bed . .2G 35
Thackeray Cl.
  CV10: Gall C 5G 21
Thames Cl. CV12: Bulk 2C 36
Thirlmere Av. CV11: Nun 3B 24
Thirlmere Rd. CV12: Bed 3E 35
  LE10: Hinc 1A 26
Thomas St. CV12: Bed 3E 35
Thorncliffe Way
  CV10: Ans C 1E 21
Thornfield Av.
  CV13: Stoke G 2G 15
Thornfield Way LE10: Hinc . .1E 27
Thornhill Dr. CV11: Nun 3D 32
Thorntons Way CV10: Nun . .6G 21
Thornycroft Rd.
  LE10: Hinc 1E 27
Three Pots Rd.
  LE10: Burb 5E 27
Thurlaston La. LE9: Earl S . . .4F 9
Thurlow Cl. CV9: Ath 3D 4
Tilton Rd. LE10: Burb 3E 27
Tintagel Way CV11: Nun 4C 24
Tintern Way CV12: Bed 3G 35
Tippett Cl. CV11: Nun 4C 32
Tithe Cl. CV13: Stoke G 3F 15
Tiverton Dr. CV11: Nun 4A 24
Toler Rd. CV10: Nun 4F 23
Tom Eatough Ct. LE9: Earl S . .5E 9
Tom Ellis Ct. CV7: Exh 5D 34
Tomkinson Rd. CV10: Nun . . .5C 22
Topp's Dr. CV12: Bed 4C 34

Topp's Heath CV12: Bed 4C 34
Top Rd. CV7: Barn 5C 36
Torridon Way LE10: Hinc 6B 16
Tourist Info. Cen.
  Nuneaton 5G 23
Tower Rd. CV12: Bed 3E 35
  LE9: Earl S 5D 8
Tower Vw. Cres.
  CV10: Nun 6H 21
Townend Rd. LE9: Barw 6G 7
Townsend Dr. CV11: Nun . . .1B 32
Townsend Rd.
  LE9: S Stan 6H 19
Townsends Cl.
  CV11: Burt H 2H 33
Trafford Cl. CV9: Ath 3D 4
Trafford Dr. CV10: Nun 4A 22
Trafford Rd. LE10: Hinc 5F 17
Tregorrick Rd. CV7: Exh 6E 35
Tregullan Rd. CV7: Exh 5F 35
Trelawney Rd. CV7: Exh 6E 35
Trenance Rd. CV7: Exh 5F 35
Treneere Rd. CV7: Exh 5F 35
Trentham Cl. CV11: Nun 3B 32
Trentham Rd.
  CV10: Harts 5G 11
Trent Rd. CV11: Nun 4H 23
  CV12: Bulk 3C 36
  LE10: Hinc 1A 26
Tresillian Rd. CV7: Exh 5F 35
Treviscoe Cl. CV7: Exh 6E 35
Trevor Rd. LE10: Hinc 6F 17
Trevose Av. CV7: Exh 6F 35
Trewint Cl. CV7: Exh 5E 35
Trident Bus. Pk.
  CV11: Nun 6H 23
Trinity Cl. LE10: Hinc 1C 26
Trinity La. LE10: Hinc 1C 26
Trinity Vicarage Rd.
  LE10: Hinc 1C 26
Trinity Wlk. CV11: Nun 6A 24
Troon Way LE10: Burb 4D 26
Truro Cl. CV11: Nun 4B 24
  LE10: Hinc 3E 17
Tryan Rd. CV10: Nun 5C 22
Tuckey Cl. LE9: Sap 1H 29
Tudor Cl. CV7: Exh 6C 34
Tudor Cres. CV9: Ath 4D 4
Tudor Rd. CV10: Nun 5C 16
Tulliver Cl. CV12: Bed 1F 35
Tulliver Rd. CV10: Nun 3G 31
Tunnel Rd. CV10: Ansl 6C 20
Turnberry Dr. CV11: Nun 3E 32
Turner Cl. CV12: Bed 1E 35
Turner Dr. LE10: Hinc 4A 16
Turville Cl. LE10: Burb 4F 27
Tuttle Hill CV10: Nun 2C 22
Tuttle Hill Ind. Est.
  CV10: Nun 2C 22
Tweedside Cl. LE10: Hinc . . .4F 17
Twycross Rd. LE10: Burb . . .3F 27
Twyford Ct. LE9: Barw 6H 7

Ullswater Av. CV11: Nun 3B 24
Ullswater Cl. LE9: Earl S 6D 8
Ullswater Rd. CV12: Bed 3E 35
Underwood Cres.
  LE9: Sap 1H 29
Underwood Dr.
  LE9: S Stan 6G 19
Unit Ind. Est. LE10: Hinc . . .3A 26
Up. Abbey St. CV11: Nun 4F 23
Up. Bond St. LE10: Hinc 6D 16
Upton Dr. CV11: Nun 3B 32
Upton La. CV13: Stoke G 2E 15

Vale Vw. CV10: Nun 5C 22
Valley Rd. CV10: Gall C 5E 21
Valliant Cl. LE10: Burb 5E 27

Veasey Cl. CV11: Nun 6A 24
Ventnor St. CV10: Nun 3H 23
Venture Ct. LE10: Hinc 1G 25
Vernons Ct. CV10: Nun 5C 22
Vernons La. CV10: Nun 5C 22
  CV11: Nun 5C 22
Verona Cl. CV10: Nun 2C 32
Vicarage Cl. CV9: Ath 6E 5
Vicarage Ct. LE9: Earl S 5D 8
Vicarage La. CV7: Ash G 6A 34
Vicarage St. CV11: Nun 5H 23
  LE9: Earl S 5D 8
Victoria Rd. CV9: Man 1F 11
  CV10: Harts 1H 21
  LE10: Burb 4F 27
Victoria St. CV11: Nun 5G 23
  LE10: Hinc 6D 16
Vilia Cl. LE10: Burb 5F 27
Villa Cl. CV12: Bulk 4D 36
Villa Cres. CV12: Bulk 4E 37
Villiers St. CV11: Nun 6F 23
Violet Cl. CV12: Bed 3C 34
Virginia Pl. CV10: Nun 6C 22

Wadebridge Dr.
  CV11: Nun 5A 24
WAGON OVERTHROW 6E 35
Wagstaff Dr. CV10: Nun 2G 21
Wakeford Cl.
  CV10: Ridge L 4A 10
Wakehurst Cl. CV11: Nun . . .3B 32
Walcote Cl. LE10: Hinc 1H 25
Walkers Way CV12: Bed 4D 34
Wallingford Av.
  CV11: Nun 2B 24
Walney Cl. LE10: Hinc 6B 16
Walnut Cl. CV10: Harts 1G 21
  CV10: Nun 3C 22
Walsingham Dr.
  CV10: Griff 3E 31
Walter Scott Rd.
  CV12: Bed 4G 35
Waltham Cres. CV10: Nun . . .5H 21
Walton Cl. CV11: Nun 4C 32
Warwick Dr. CV9: Ath 3D 4
Warwick Gdns.
  CV10: Nun 6C 22
  LE10: Hinc 4E 17
Warwick Grn. CV12: Bulk . . .4E 37
Washington St. LE9: Barw . . .1G 17
Waste La. CV9: Gren, Ath 4A 4
Waterfall Way LE9: Barw 2F 17
Waterfield Way
  LE10: Burb 4B 26
Waterloo Rd. LE10: Hinc 1C 26
Watersbridge Gdns.
  CV11: Nun 2G 31
Waters End LE9: Barw 2G 17
Watling Cl. LE10: Burb 5C 26
Watling Ct. CV11: Nun 6A 24
Watling Dr. LE10: Burb 5C 26
Watling St.
  CV9: Gren, Ath 3A 4
  CV9: Man, Wthn 6F 5
  CV10: Cald, Harts 3D 12
  CV10: Nun 5H 13
  CV10: Nun 5H 13
Waveney Cl. LE10: Hinc 1A 26
Waverley Av. CV11: Nun 2A 32
Waverley Sq. CV11: Nun 3B 32
Weaver Rd. LE9: Earl S 5E 9
Webb St. CV10: Nun 6A 22
Webbs Way LE9: S Stan 5H 19
WEDDINGTON 2G 23
Weddington Ind. Est.
  CV10: Nun 4G 23
Weddington La.
  CV10: Nun, Cald 3E 13
Weddington Ter.
  CV10: Nun 4H 23
Welbeck Av. LE10: Burb 5D 26
Welcome St. CV9: Ath 5E 5
Wellington Cl. LE10: Burb . . .5E 27